# JOHN OF THE CROSS

**THE CROSSROAD SPIRITUAL LEGACY SERIES**
Edited by John Farina

# JOHN OF THE CROSS

## DOCTOR OF LIGHT AND LOVE

*Kieran Kavanaugh, O.C.D.*

A Crossroad Book
The Crossroad Publishing Company
New York

The Crossroad Publishing Company
481 Eighth Avenue, New York, NY 10001

Printed in the United States of America

*Library of Congress Cataloging-in-Publication Data*

Kavanaugh, Kieran, 1928–
    John of the Cross : doctor of light and love / Kieran Kavanaugh.
        p.    cm. — (The crossroad spiritual legacy series)
    ISBN 0-8245-2515-9 (pbk.)
    1. John of the Cross, Saint, 1542–1591.    2. Christian saints—
Spain. Biography.    I. Title.    II. Series.
BX4700.J7K38    1999
271'.7302—dc21
    [B]                                                99-33217
                                                        CIP

# Contents

# Foreword

John of the Cross is probably best known for the term "Dark Night of the Soul." It conjures up images of severe asceticism, austerity, sacrifice, and gloom; of a terrifying encounter with a fierce, mysterious force; of a frightening moment, bordering on madness, in which the very foundation of our consciousness and well-being is assaulted. Perhaps it is good to have such an image in an age when priests have become professional nice guys and we hear incessantly, cloyingly, about how much God loves us.

But the Dark Night of the Soul, in all its terror, is not what this man John was fundamentally about. To think that he was would be like thinking that birth is only about pain, that gardening is only about plucking out weeds, or that the brilliance of noon is only a prelude to night. Suffering was indeed part of John, who changed his religious name from Juan de Santo Matía to Juan de la Cruz to reflect his devotion to the cross. He was born into a poor family in Castile in the middle of the sixteenth century. He lost his parents early. He was imprisoned for months by his fellow believers in a windowless closet next to a latrine. In the prime of his life he lost favor with some of the leaders of his own reform movement who wished to send him into the obscurity of the missions in Mexico. He died at the age of forty-nine.

The chiaroscuro needs to be balanced lest we not see beyond the cicatrices and the pain. John was a charismatic leader of a religious and social movement that inspired hundreds of men and women from all classes to strike out to form alternative communities based on charity, cooperation, simplicity, and harmony with nature. He was a skilled counselor to scores of men and women in an age before highly paid psychiatrists. He administered monasteries, which were complex economies that depended significantly on their own industry for survival. He was an entrepreneur and builder who bought lands, planned buildings, mortared walls, and cultivated gardens. He was a professor who taught students and reasoned with the learned. And most importantly for us, he was an author who wrote both theological treatises of such scholarly refinement that he was declared a Doctor of the Church and such fresh, vibrant poetry that he is hailed as one of the greatest poets Spain has ever produced. He was a man of many colors, not only of black and white.

In this volume we will see the many shades, tones, and textures that make John's writings so remarkable. Kieran Kavanaugh has spent a lifetime studying John of the Cross and attempting to follow his example. We could have few more able guides to John and few more challenging, more real guides to life than John.

John Farina

# Preface

Whoever delves into St. John of the Cross begins soon to realize what a bountiful treasure lies there, but it is a treasure difficult to mine. The effort to draw out its riches has left us with an extensive literature in the Spanish language consisting of commentary and critical studies. Such studies in English are relatively rare. On the other hand, many of those interested in John's message are not desirous of spending time on the fine points and meticulous presentations of critical research.

I am happy, then, to have this opportunity from The Crossroad Publishing Company to present John of the Cross to English-speaking readers in accordance with the design of its Spiritual Legacy Series. The texts of John of the Cross themselves will constitute the more important aspect of this book, filling the commentary with life as does the soul for the body.

In choosing a particular framework in which to view John's teaching, I am at the same time fully aware that any number of others could be devised. An explanation of some of the thought forms of John's times, some of the philosophy used by him that people are unfamiliar with, seemed a necessary part of my task to assist readers to understand him correctly. But principally this commentary flows from my own experience and that of many other spiritual seekers I have come to know through the years. Such experience is obviously limited. But it is a means I have found useful for gauging the needs and questions of present-day readers.

It takes a certain amount of daring to write commentary on an author as rich and profound as John of the Cross. I cannot help but think of Jonathan Swift's Lemuel Gulliver, who in Glubbdudrib proposed that Homer and Aristotle might appear at the head of all their commentators. The commentators were so numerous that there was no room for them all in the palace. Gulliver soon discovered that the commentators always kept in the most distant quarters from their principals in shame and guilt because they had so horribly misrepresented the meaning of these authors to posterity.

I, though, must admit my gratitude to the many commentators on John from whom I have benefited. Since this book is not meant for academics and did not call for mention of sources or critical comment on other studies, I want to express here my gratefulness to a number of Spanish sanjuanist scholars by whose writings I have been influenced and enlightened over the years: Secundino Castro, Miguel A. Diez, Eulogio Pacho, Federico Ruiz, and Juan Saera. The bibliography will supply the reader with a selected list of books on John of the Cross published in English.

I owe much to the members and participants in the Carmelite Forum, which has been sponsored now for twelve summers by the Center for Spirituality at Saint Mary's College, Notre Dame, Indiana, under the direction of Dr. Keith J. Egan. The interaction among the presenters and participants has proved a remarkable stimulus and opportunity for exchange with people from many backgrounds. Study and reflection together in a prayerful atmosphere have provided us with rewarding opportunities to learn from one another, receive new insights and grow in our understanding of John.

I am deeply grateful to Carol Lisi and Marc Foley for reading my manuscript and helping me with their suggestions, alerting me to many passages that needed clarification, expansion, or rewording. I would like to thank as well the members of the Institute of Carmelite Studies for their support and encouragement in the Teresian studies with which I am at present engaged. Finally I am grateful to I.C.S. Publications for allowing me to quote so amply from *The Collected Works of St. John of the Cross.*

# Abbreviations

# Poems

## Cántico Espíritual

Canciones entre el alma y el Esposo

*Esposa*
1. ¿Adónde te escondiste,
Amado, y me dejaste con gemido?
Como el ciervo huiste,
habiéndome herido;
salí tras ti clamando, y eras ido.

2. Pastores los que fuerdes
allá por las majadas al otero,
si por ventura vierdes
aquel que yo más quiero,
decilde que adolezco, peno y muero.

3. Buscando mis amores,
iré por esos montes y riberas;
ni cogeré las flores,
ni temeré las fieras,
y pasaré los fuertes y fronteras.

4. ¡Oh bosques y espesuras,
plantadas por la mano del Amado!
¡Oh prado de verduras,
de flores esmaltado,
decid si por vosotros ha pasado!

# Poems

## The Spiritual Canticle

Songs between the soul and the Bridegroom

*Bride*
1. Where have you hidden,
Beloved, and left me moaning?
You fled like the stag
after wounding me;
I went out calling you, but you were gone.

2. Shepherds, you that go
up through the sheepfolds to the hill,
if by chance you see
him I love most,
tell him that I am sick, I suffer, and I die.

3. Seeking my love
I will head for the mountains and for watersides;
I will not gather flowers,
nor fear wild beasts;
I will go beyond strong men and frontiers.

4. O woods and thickets
planted by the hand of my Beloved!
O green meadow,
coated, bright, with flowers,
tell me, has he passed by you?

5. Mil gracias derramando
pasó por estos sotos con presura,
y, yéndolos mirando,
con sola su figura,
vestidos los dejó de hermosura.

6. ¡Ay, quién podrá sanarme!
¡Acaba de entregarte ya de vero;
no quieras enviarme
de hoy más ya mensajero
que no saben decirme lo que quiero!

7. Y todos cuantos vagan
de ti me van mil gracias refiriendo,
y todos más me llagan,
y déjeme muriendo
un no sé qué que quedan balbuciendo.

8. Mas ¿como perseveras,
¡oh vida!, no viviendo donde vives,
y haciendo porque mueras
las flechas que recibes
de lo que del Amado en ti concibes?

9. ¿Por qué, pues has llagado
aqueste corazón, no le sanaste?
Y, pues me le has robado,
¿por qué así le dejaste,
y no tomas el robo que robaste?

10. ¡Apaga mis enojos,
pues que ninguno basta a deshacellos,
y véante mis ojos,
pues eres lumbre dellos,
y sólo para ti quiero tenellos!

5. Pouring out a thousand graces,
he passed these groves in haste;
and having looked at them,
with his image alone,
clothed them in beauty.

6. Ah, who has the power to heal me?
Now wholly surrender yourself!
Do not send me
any more messengers;
they cannot tell me what I must hear.

7. All who are free
tell me a thousand graceful things of you;
all wound me more
and leave me dying
of, ah, I-don't-know-what behind their stammering.

8. How do you endure
O life, not living where you live,
and being brought near death
by the arrows you receive
from that which you conceive of your Beloved?

9. Why, since you wounded
this heart, don't you heal it?
And why, since you stole it from me,
do you leave it so,
and fail to carry off what you have stolen?

10. Extinguish these miseries,
since no one else can stamp them out;
and may my eyes behold you,
because you are their light,
and I would open them to you alone.

11. Descubre tu presencia
y máteme tu vista y hermosura
mira que la dolencia
de amor, que no se cura
sino con la presencia y la figura.

12. ¡Oh cristalina fuente,
si en esos tus semblantes plateados
formases de repente
los ojos deseados
que tengo en mis entrañas dibujados!

13. ¡Apártalos, Amado,
que voy de vuelo!

*Esposo*
   —Vuélvate, paloma,
que el ciervo vulnerado
por el otero asoma
al aire de tu vuelo, y fresco toma!

*Esposa*
14. Mi Amado, las montañas,
los valles solitarios nemorosos,
las ínsulas extrañas,
los ríos sonorosos,
el silbo de los aires amorosos,

15. la noche sosegada
en par de los levantes aurora,
la música callada,
la soledad sonora,
la cena que recrea y enamora.

16. Cazadnos las raposas,
que está ya florecida nuestra viña,

11. Reveal your presence,
and may the vision of your beauty be my death;
for the sickness of love
is not cured
except by your very presence and image.

12. O spring like crystal!
If only, on your silvered-over faces,
you would suddenly form
the eyes I have desired,
which I bear sketched deep within my heart.

13. Withdraw them, Beloved,
I am taking flight!

*Bridegroom*
  —Return, dove,
the wounded stag
is in sight on the hill,
cooled by the breeze of your flight.

*The Bride*
14. My Beloved, the mountains,
and lonely wooded valleys,
strange islands,
and resounding rivers,
the whistling of love-stirring breezes,

15. the tranquil night
at the time of the rising dawn,
silent music,
sounding solitude,
the supper that refreshes, and deepens love.

16. Catch us the foxes,
for our vineyard is now in flower,

en tanto que de rosas
hacemos una piña,
y no parezca nadie en la montiña.

17. Detente, cierzo muerto;
ven, austro, que recuerdas los amores,
aspira por mi huerto,
y corran sus olores,
y pacerá el Amado entre las flores.

18. ¡Oh ninfas de Judea!
en tanto que en las flores y rosales
el ámbar perfumea,
morá en los arrabales,
y no queráis tocar nuestros umbrales.

19. Escóndete, Carillo,
y mira con tu haz a las montañas,
y no quieras decillo;
mas mira las compañas
de la que va por ínsulas extrañas.

*Esposo*
20. A las aves ligeras,
leones, ciervos, gamos saltadores,
montes, valles, riberas,
aguas, aires, ardores,
y miedos de las noches veladores:

21. por las amenas liras
y canto de serenas os conjuro
que cesen vuestras iras,
y no toquéis al muro,
porque la esposa duerma más seguro.

while we fashion a cone of roses
intricate as the pine's;
and let no one appear on the hill.

17. Be still, deadening north wind; south wind
come, you that waken love,
breathe through my garden,
let its fragrance flow,
and the Beloved will feed amid the flowers.

18. You girls of Judea,
while among flowers and roses
the amber spreads its perfume,
stay away, there on the outskirts:
do not so much as seek to touch our thresholds.

19. Hide yourself, my love;
turn your face toward the mountains,
and do not speak;
but look at those companions
going with her through strange islands.

*Bridegroom*
20. Swift-winged birds,
lions, stags, and leaping roes,
mountains, lowlands, and river banks,
waters, winds, and ardors,
watching fears of night:

21. By the pleasant lyres
and the siren's song, I conjure you
to cease your anger
and not touch the wall,
that the bride may sleep in deeper peace.

22. Entrado se ha la esposa
en el ameno huerto deseado,
y a su sabor reposa,
el cuello reclinado
sobre los dulces brazos del Amado.

23. Debajo del manzano,
allí conmigo fuiste desposada;
allí te di la mano
y fuiste reparada
donde tu madre fuera violada.

*Esposa*
24. Nuestro lecho florido,
de cuevas de leones enlazado,
en púrpura tendido,
de paz edificado,
de mil escudos de oro coronado.

25. A zaga de tu huella
las jóvenes discurren al camino,
al toque de centella,
al adobado vino,
emisiones de bálsamo divino.

26.. En la interior bodega
de mi Amado bebí, y cuando salía
por toda aquesta vega,
ya cosa no sabía;
y el ganado perdí que antes seguía.

27. Allí me dio su pecho,
allí me enseñó ciencia muy sabrosa;
y yo le di de hecho
a mí, sin dejar cosa;
allí le prometí de ser su esposa.

22. The bride has entered
the sweet garden of her desire,
and she rests in delight,
laying her neck
on the gentle arms of her Beloved.

23. Beneath the apple tree:
there I took you for my own,
there I offered you my hand,
and restored you,
where your mother was corrupted.

*Bride*
24. Our bed is in flower,
bound round with linking dens of lions,
hung with purple,
built up in peace,
and crowned with a thousand shields of gold.

25. Following your footprints,
maidens run along the way;
the touch of a spark,
the spiced wine,
cause flowings in them from the balsam of God.

26. In the inner wine cellar
I drank of my Beloved, and, when I went abroad
through all this valley,
I no longer knew anything,
and lost the herd that I was following.

27. There he gave me his breast;
there he taught me a sweet and living knowledge;
and I gave myself to him,
keeping nothing back;
there I promised to be his bride.

28. Mi alma se ha empleado,
y todo mi caudal en su servicio;
ya no guardo ganado,
ni ya tengo otro oficio,
que ya sólo en amar es mi ejercicio.

29. Pues ya si en el ejido
de hoy más no fuere vista ni hallada,
diréis que me he perdido;
que, andando enamorada,
me hice perdidiza y fui ganada.

30. De flores y esmeraldas,
en las frescas mañanas escogidas,
haremos las guirnaldas
en tu amor florecidas
y en un cabello mío entretejidas.

31. En solo aquel cabello
que en mi cuello volar consideraste,
mirástele en mi cuello,
y en él preso quedaste,
y en uno de mis ojos te llagaste.

32. Cuando tú me mirabas
su gracia en mí tus ojos imprimían;
por eso me adamabas,
y en eso merecían
los míos adorar lo que en ti vían.

33. No quieras despreciarme,
que, si color moreno en mí hallaste,
ya bien puedes mirarme
después que me miraste,
que gracia y hermosura en mí dejaste.

28. Now I occupy my soul
and all my energy in his service;
I no longer tend the herd,
nor have I any other work
now that my every act is love.

29. If, then, I am no longer
seen or found on the common,
you will say that I am lost;
that, stricken by love,
I lost myself, and was found.

30. With flowers and emeralds
chosen on cool mornings
we shall weave garlands
flowering in your love,
and bound with one hair of mine.

31. You considered
that one hair fluttering at my neck;
you gazed at it upon my neck
and it captivated you;
and one of my eyes wounded you.

32. When you looked at me
your eyes imprinted your grace in me;
for this you loved me ardently;
and thus my eyes deserved
to adore what they beheld in you.

33. Do not despise me;
for if, before, you found me dark,
now truly you can look at me
since you have looked
and left in me grace and beauty.

*Esposo*
34. La blanca palomica
al arca con el ramo se ha tornado;
y ya la tortolica
al socio deseado
en las riberas verdes ha hallado.

35. En soledad vivía,
y en soldedad ha puesto ya su nido,
y en soledad la guía
a solas su querido,
también en soledad de amor herido.

*Esposa*
36. Gocémonos, Amado,
y vámonos a ver en tu hermosura
al monte y al collado
do mana el agua pura;
entremos más adentro en la espesura,

37. Y luego a las subidas
cavernas de la piedra nos iremos,
que están bien escondidas,
y allí nos entraremos,
y el mosto de granadas gustaremos.

38. Allí me mostrarías
aquello que mi alma pretendía,
y luego me darías
allí, tú, ¡vida mía!
aquello que me diste el otro día:

39. El aspirar del aire,
el canto de la dulce filomena,
el soto y su donaire,

*Bridegroom*
34. The small white dove
has returned to the ark with an olive branch;
and now the turtledove
has found its longed-for mate
by the green river banks.

35. She lived in solitude,
and now in solitude has built her nest;
and in solitude he guides her,
he alone, who also bears
in solitude the wound of love.

*Bride*
36. Let us rejoice, Beloved,
and let us go forth to behold ourselves in your beauty,
to the mountain and to the hill,
to where the pure water flows,
and further, deep into the thicket.

37. And then we will go on
to the high caverns in the rock
which are so well concealed;
there we shall enter
and taste the fresh juice of the pomegranates.

38. There you will show me
what my soul has been seeking,
and then you will give me,
you, my life, will give me there
what you gave me on that other day:

39. the breathing of the air,
the song of the sweet nightingale;
the grove and its living beauty

en la noche serena,
con llama que consume y no da pena.

40. Que nadie lo miraba;
Aminadab tampoco parecía
y el cerco sosegaba
y la caballería
a vista de las aguas descendía.

# Noche Oscura

Canciones de el alma que se goza de haber llegado
al alto estado de la perfección, que es la unión con
Dios, por el camino de la negación espiritual.

1. En un noche oscura,
con ansias, en amores inflamada,
¡oh dichosa ventura!
salí sin ser notada
estando ya me casa sosegada.

2. A oscuras y segura,
por la secreta escala disfrazada,
¡oh dichosa ventura!
a oscuras y en celada,
estando ya mi casa sosegada.

3. En la noche dichosa,
en secreto, que nadie me veía,
ni yo miraba cosa,
sin otra luz y quía
sino la que en el corazón ardía.

4. Aquésta me guiaba
más cierto que la luz del mediodía,

in the serene night,
with a flame that is consuming and painless.

40. No one looked at her,
nor did Aminadab appear;
the siege was still;
and the cavalry,
at the sight of the waters, descended.

# The Dark Night

Songs of the soul that rejoices in having reached the
high state of perfection, which is union with God,
by the path of spiritual negation.

1. One dark night,
fired with love's urgent longings
—ah, the sheer grace!—
I went out unseen,
my house being now all stilled.

2. In darkness, and secure,
by the secret ladder, disguised,
—ah, the sheer grace!—
in darkness and concealment,
my house being now all stilled.

3. On that glad night
in secret, for no one saw me,
nor did I look at anything
with no other light or guide
than the one that burned in my heart.

4. This guided me
more surely than the light of noon

adónde me esperaba
quien yo bien me sabía,
en parte donde nadie parecía.

5. ¡Oh noche que guiaste!
¡Oh noche amable más que el alborada!
¡Oh noche que juntaste
Amado con amada,
amada en el Amado transformada!

6. En mi pecho florido,
que entero para él solo se guardaba,
allí quedó dormido,
y yo le regalaba,
y el ventalle de cedros aire daba.

7. El aire de la almena,
cuando yo sus cabellos esparcía,
con su mano serena
en mi cuello hería
y todos mis sentidos suspendía.

8. Quedéme y olvidéme,
el rostro recliné sobre el Amado,
cesó todo y dejéme,
dejando me cuidado
entre las azucenas olvidado.

to where he was awaiting me
—him I knew so well—
there in a place where no one appeared.

5. O guiding night!
O night more lovely than the dawn!
O night that has united
the Lover with his beloved,
transforming the beloved in her Lover.

6. Upon my flowering breast,
which I kept wholly for him alone,
there he lay sleeping,
and I caressing him
there in a breeze from the fanning cedars.

7. When the breeze blew from the turret,
as I parted his hair,
it wounded my neck
with its gentle hand,
suspending all my senses.

8. I abandoned and forgot myself,
laying my face on my Beloved;
all things ceased; I went out from myself,
leaving my cares
forgotten among the lilies.

# Llama de Amor Viva

Canciones del alma en la intima communicación de unión de amor de Dios.

1. ¡Oh llama de amor viva,
que tiernamente hieres
de mi alma en el más profundo centro!
Pues ya no eres esquiva,
acaba ya, si quieres;
¡rompe la tela de este dulce encuentro!

2. ¡Oh cauterio suave!
¡Oh regalada llaga!
¡Oh mano blanda! ¡Oh toque delicado,
que a vida eterna sabe,
y toda deuda paga!
Matando, muerte en vida la has trocado.

3. ¡Oh lámparas de fuego,
en cuyos resplandores
las profundas cavernas del sentido,
que estaba oscuro y ciego,
con extraños primores
calor y luz dan junto a su Querido!

4. ¡Cuán manso y amoroso
recuerdas en mi seno,
donde secretamente solo moras,
y en tu aspirar sabroso,
de bien y gloria lleno,
cuán delicadamente me enamoras!

# The Living Flame of Love

Songs of the soul in the intimate communication of loving union with God.

1. O living flame of love
that tenderly wounds my soul
in its deepest center! Since
now you are not oppressive,
now consummate! If it be your will:
tear through the veil of this sweet encounter!

2. O sweet cautery,
O delightful wound!
O gentle hand! O delicate touch
that tastes of eternal life
and pays every debt!
In killing you changed death to life.

3. O lamps of fire!
in whose splendors
the deep caverns of feeling,
once obscure and blind,
now give forth, so rarely, so exquisitely,
both warmth and light to their Beloved.

4. How gently and lovingly
you wake in my heart,
where in secret you dwell alone;
and in your sweet breathing,
filled with good and glory,
how tenderly you swell my heart with love.

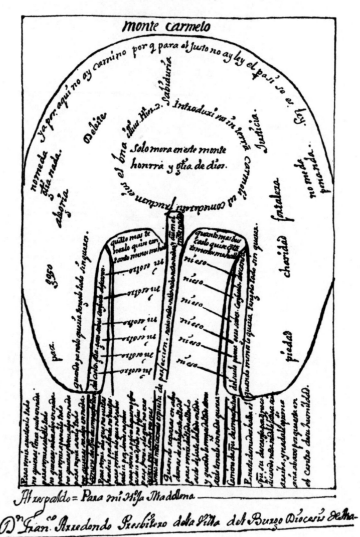

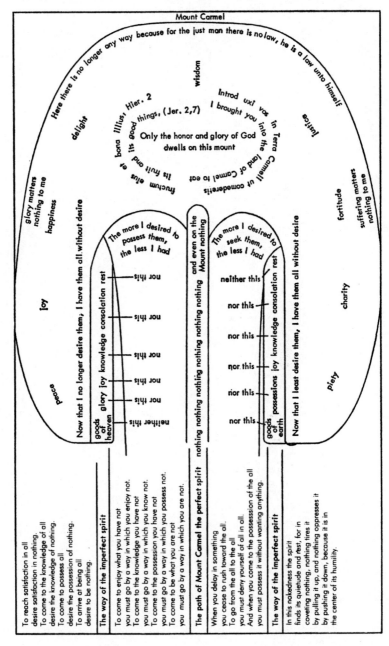

# Chapter 1

# A Troubadour of Divine Love

*49 years old*

On the evening of 13 December 1591 in the little town of Ubeda in the south of Spain, Fray John of the Cross lay dying in his monastery while the community gathered at his bedside. His prior, after fumbling through a book of prayers, began the melancholy recitation for the commendation of a soul. The small friar interrupted and asked the prior to read instead from the Song of Songs. Then, listening to its poetry, to its exotic lines of love, he exclaimed: "Oh, what precious pearls!" The words spoke to Fray John like no others of the love he had come to know within the trinitarian mystery where he now found his rest, sharing in the communion of Persons in God. Who would have thought of asking for something like this? But who could have written so sublimely of love as John of the Cross?

Once the soul is placed at the peak of perfection and freedom of spirit in God, and all the repugnances and contradictions of sensuality have ceased, she no longer has any other activity to engage her than surrender to the delights and joys of intimate love of her Bridegroom. . . . Let us rejoice in the communication of the sweetness of love, not only in that sweetness we already possess in our habitual union but in that which overflows into the effective and actual practice of love, either interiorly with the will in the affective act or exteriorly in works directed to the service of the Beloved. . . . [W]hen love takes root it has this characteristic: It makes one always desire to taste the joys and sweetnesses of love in the inward and outward exercise of love. All this the lover does in order to resemble the Beloved more. (C 36.1.3)

For all their beauty and power John's words were not what mainly interested his earliest biographers. It was later that history came to recognize this saint as a troubadour of divine love. Biographers of persons who were renowned for holiness exalted the venerable in their subjects and were judged successful if beatification soon followed publication of their accounts. A saint had to be presented as heroic in a way that would meet the baroque mold of the time. The demands were for the marvelous, the miraculous, the spectacular—and the more reportable incidents of this type the better. Tales of the ordinary, of all that the saints might have in common with the rest of humanity, were not worth paper or ink. Through the centuries, then, history's portrait makers have interpreted John in changing light. First he was drawn darkly, an ascetic, an austere and emaciated man, laudably surrounded by miracles, with a rather forbidding doctrine. To this sketch was later added a wash of mysticism. His books could not be recommended or even intelligible except to those rare persons walking the path of penance, sufferers of that dismal affliction called the "dark night of the soul." The picture of John as ascetic and mystic persisted for centuries, and perhaps, here and there, an image like this still lingers.

Not until the twentieth century did John of the Cross, in a new stroke of the brush, receive recognition for something further. He was pronounced a Doctor of the Church and so was acknowledged as a theologian, a master especially in spirituality. Next, literary critics began to admit that the verses of his poetry, saturated with a prodigality of symbols, amounted to more than mere devotional rhymes. Menendez y Pelayo, among others, commented:

> Here we are faced with an evangelical poetry, both heavenly and divine, so much so that one gets the feeling that it does not belong to this earth. . . . I confess that these verses fill me with a religious awe when I handle them. Here the Spirit of God has passed, embellishing and sanctifying everything.

From the new image of John as Mystical Doctor, theologian, and poet, the interest then shifted to the material, economic, and moral responsibilities he carried.

But in all of these images John of the Cross remains the great lover of God. In his apostolic letter *Master of Faith*, written to commemorate the fourth centenary of John's death, Pope John Paul II states:

> St. John of the Cross had fallen deeply in love with God. He had great familiarity with God and always spoke to him and of him. God was in his heart and on his lips, because God was his true treasure, his true world. Before proclaiming and singing the mystery of God, he was a witness of God; he used to speak of God with a fervor and conviction which were remarkably exceptional.

John lived in Spain during the sixteenth century, now called its golden age, a period of broad European expansion. Spain, and Portugal as well, was discovering the new world with its "strange islands," which inspired John's phrase. El Greco in Toledo was painting his mystical figures. Garcilaso de la Vega, Luis de León, and Cervantes were dominating the world of Spanish literature. It was a time also when the Italian Renaissance had reached exalted heights exemplified in the masterpieces of Leonardo da Vinci, Michelangelo, and Raphael. In England, William Shakespeare like no one else entered the domain of drama, channeling the English language into whirls and eddies of poetic beauty. The Copernican revolution was in process. And within Christianity the movement of reform was mounting, with serious ruptures and conflicts under way initiated by Luther, Calvin, the Huguenots, the Council of Trent, and St. Ignatius Loyola, founder of the Jesuits.

### Early Years

Juan de Yepes Alvarez (the future John of the Cross) was born in a little town some thirty miles north of Avila in 1542. His father, Gonzalo de Yepes, belonging to a family of silk merchants, of Jewish background it seems now, was disinherited for having entered a marriage of love with a poor woman. She was Catalina Alvarez, perhaps of Arab origins, an orphan who subsisted as a silk weaver. Compelled to live in poverty, the couple experienced hardships so severe that Gonzalo died before their three sons, Francisco, Luis, and Juan, were old enough to care for themselves.

Little Juan de Yepes, along with the many other poor of Spain, from the very beginning suffered in the shadow of the cross. In contrast with the sprawling, outward glitter of the political leadership, the conditions of life for Castilians were markedly different. Life was fragile. The median age at time of death was twenty-seven years, and plagues, epidemics, and hunger preyed unmercifully on children, those of the poor especially. Juan's brother Luis died as a child.

Struggling to provide the basics of life for the family, Catalina moved first to Arévalo and then to Medina del Campo, known for its large trade and busy marketplaces. Juan de Yepes lived thirteen years in Medina, from age nine to twenty-two. He was one of those saints, like St. Thérèse of Lisieux, who from childhood center their lives on God. His mother said that as a child he was like an angel. And St. Teresa wrote of him, "he is a saint and always was one." Fortunately Catalina was able to enroll him in a school for children of the poor, where he could receive an elementary education and learn a trade. But Juan was more interested in books than in trades.

One of his tasks at this time was to assist dutifully for several hours each day at the church of *La Magdalena* attached to a monastery of nuns. There he was noticed by Don Alonso de Toledo, administrator of a charity hospital for those suffering from venereal disease. Juan was recruited by him to help care for the sick and also to go about begging alms for the hospital. Here Catalina's son came into direct contact with human misery and much of its stench, and in his work as a beggar learned to withstand scorn and rejection. Observing the young lad's talent, his love of books, and his dedication to the disagreeable tasks meted out to him in the hospital, the administrator allowed Juan to attend classes at the Jesuit "school of grammar," where the principal subject of Latin was rounded out by other courses such as rhetoric, theology, mathematics, history, geography. There were also competitive exercises and theatrical productions of the classics. Don Alonso was so pleased with Juan's assiduousness in all these duties that he wanted him to continue studies preparatory to ordination and become chaplain at the hospital.

## A Carmelite Call

Juan surprised both the administrator and the Jesuits by deciding in the end to enter the Carmelite monastery of friars in Medina. The history of this order goes back to the early thirteenth century, when hermits lived and prayed on Mount Carmel in the Holy Land and dedicated their church to Mary. As a Carmelite, Juan was given the name Fray Juan de Santo Matía. During his one-year novitiate he learned about the traditions and spirituality of Carmel. After making his profession of vows, he was sent to Salamanca to study at the university there, a school on a par with others in the great medieval tradition—Bologna, Oxford, Paris. Juan spent four intense years studying in this flourishing intellectual center, immersed in its art and culture, and in the swirling debates set off by stimulating new ideas. So successful was he in his studies that in his monastery he was appointed prefect of studies. This entailed teaching some classes, defending public theses, and collaborating with his teacher in answering objections to these theses.

Despite his success, Fray Juan de Santo Matía experienced dissatisfaction with his situation. The academic life did not attract him; it focused too exclusively on the purposeless splendor of a grand display of titles, promotions, offices, and professorships. He was drawn instead to contemplation in solitude before the Blessed Sacrament.

## A Change of Direction

At this time an extraordinary Carmelite nun from Avila, Teresa of Jesus, was struggling to bring to a successful conclusion her second monastery of discalced nuns in Medina del Campo. Having heard about the twenty-five-year-old friar, who at the time was just newly ordained, she arranged to speak with him. It didn't take her long to discern who it was who sat on the other side of the grille conversing with her in that self-effacing way that came so naturally to him. She understood his vocation crisis and at once began pressing him to assist her in founding a monastery of discalced friars.

Teresa had lived for over twenty years at the Incarnation, a large monastery of Carmelite nuns in Avila, in which there resided at times as many as 180 nuns. They came from different rungs on the social ladder, and those on the upper rungs insisted on bringing their special privileges with them into the monastery. This great number of nuns with their class distinctions caused many obstacles to the common life of solitude, recollection, and prayer. It was difficult to discover any resemblance to the early community of hermits on Mount Carmel.

Having experienced the transforming powers of prayer, Teresa's convictions about the interior life grew so strong that she attracted others to spiritual conversation and friendship with her. Her cell at the Incarnation became a meeting place for those beginning to long for a way of life closer to the early hermits. Soon her reform took shape. Her communities would be small, resembling the twelve disciples gathered as friends around Christ. Within the framework of Carmelite cenobitical life she restored its eremitical thrust. In addition she illuminated this Carmelite ideal with fresh insight, underscoring the apostolic and ecclesial dimensions of prayer. At a time when the wars of religion in France between the Huguenots and the Catholics erupted and so many Christians were taking up arms, she reasoned that the way to restore unity to the Body of Christ was through the arms of prayer, a contemplative life lived in the service of Christ and his church. She wanted the members of her communities to be devout explorers of the mysteries of Christ, in love with him, athirst for union with him. Their days and months would be further sanctified by celebration together of the Liturgy of the Hours. They were to follow the urgings of the rule toward a love for solitude, simplicity of life, and contemplation. But in the spirit of sisterhood, they would take recreation together. With gentleness, moderation, and joy, they were to live in a poor house, consider it to be the Blessed Virgin Mary's house, whose habit they were wearing under the rule of Our Lady of Mount Carmel.

Now with authorization from the general of the Carmelite order she was searching for suitable candidates to undertake and promote her ideal among the friars. The general, however, insisted that her friars also serve their neighbor through the ministry of the word. And Teresa included spiritual direction within the sphere of this apostolic action. The followers of Teresa's way were soon called discalced Carmelites to distinguish them from other Carmelites, who were often by contrast spoken of as "calced." The popular term "discalced" eventually became a part of the official title of the Teresian reform; the term "calced" was never used officially.

### Reform Movements

These facts are grasped better if seen within their historical context, the climate of vital reform present within European Christianity. During the crisis of the black death in the fourteenth century, many adaptations and mitigations in religious life became necessary. The result was almost a complete desertion of monastic practices. The subsequent need was for reform. As a result, important persons within religious orders promoted reform. But the church hierarchy and the politically powerful monarchs and members of the nobility promoted it as well. Neither was it unusual for the laity themselves to enthusiastically back the reformers.

From the end of the fifteenth century, Castile was a hotbed of reform movements. They began during the period of the Catholic monarchs and Cardinal Cisneros and continued up to the close of the Council of Trent and the time of Philip II. Philip II thought that much of the breakup of Christian unity could be blamed on the laxity of religious orders. For him the unity of Spain depended on religious unity, and so the reform of religious orders constituted an essential part of his plans to hold Spain together and expand its fortunes.

The model of reform that most influenced Teresa was the Franciscan reform. Already in the fifteenth century the Franciscans sought to restore the observance of the vows and community life to those who had laid them aside. Those who embraced the observance were called the "observants." Those who did not were called "conventuals." A still more radical reform, however, was introduced by those called discalced Franciscans.

The orders that then chose to become discalced had common characteristics. First, there was a return to the genuine sources that were lost by mitigations of the primitive rule. The return was built on austerity. Austerities were the means in which these reforms found their identifying signs. The signs included first of all poor buildings, small in size, without the furnishings of the nobility, and located in rural settings. The members went about completely barefoot or in hemp sandals, like the poor, and were therefore called discalced. The habit was close-fitting and of poor material. They slept on hard beds and observed prolonged fasts and abstinence from meat. They frowned on studies and academic degrees, which they considered responsible for laxity and incompatible with contemplation.

### Early Stages

St. Teresa incorporated many of these elements for her nuns and friars. But as time went on she lost some of her enthusiasm for several of these external signs. Above all, she wanted contemplative friars who would also be learned spiritual directors and preachers. For this reason, the discalced Carmelite friars began to establish themselves especially in cities having universities.

Teresa convinced Fray Juan that he would be able to find just what he was looking for by living the primitive Carmelite rule according to her ideal. After he agreed to follow her, she invited him to accompany her to found a new community of her nuns in Valladolid. There he received firsthand instructions about her ideal. Except for strict enclosure, the friars would reincarnate the lifestyle already begun by Teresa's nuns at St. Joseph's in Avila and codified in *The Way of Perfection*. The friars, however, in addition chose to follow the monastic practice of breaking their sleep and sanctifying the night by reciting Matins at midnight. Teresa had elected to do this shortly after nine. While Fray Juan was in Valladolid, she designed and made for him the first habit of the discalced Carmelite friars.

The ramshackle house Teresa managed to acquire for her first foundation of friars was located in a remote and solitary place called Duruelo, not many miles from Fontiveros. The life of the discalced Carmelite friars was inaugurated on 27 November 1568. Fray Juan de Santo Matía changed his name at this time to Fray Juan de la Cruz and has been known ever since by that name—in English, John of the Cross. Because of crowded conditions in the small house, the community soon had to move to the nearby town of Mancera de Abajo. Meanwhile Teresa founded another monastery for friars in Pastrana and called on Fray John to go there and teach them her way of life as he had learned it from her.

As the number of friars attracted to the reform movement grew, so did the need for a house of studies. A house was established in Alcalá de Henares close to the acclaimed university there, and John was appointed rector in April 1571. These events coincided with the decision of the apostolic visitor Pedro Fernández to order Teresa of Jesus, over her strong protests, to return as prioress to her original monastery of the Incarnation, where her leadership and spirituality were much needed as remedy to the problems that resulted from years of inept administration. Convinced that she needed expert help for the challenges that lay ahead, she persuaded Pedro Fernández to appoint John of the Cross as confessor and vicar of the monastery. Teresa explained the change to the nuns simply: "I am bringing as your confessor a father who is a saint."

## Conflicts of Jurisdiction

How did Pedro Fernández, a Dominican friar, acquire such authority? To understand this we need to understand King Philip II's distrust of the methods for reform of religious orders set up in Rome. He wanted to take over in Spain and refused to hear of reforms of Spanish monasteries carried on by those he considered outsiders, the orders' generals coming from Rome. His vehement desire was to force all religious "conventual" communities into "observants."

From Pius V he received authority in 1566 to instruct the Spanish bishops to carry out visitations of religious orders. These visitations were to be done through delegates who in turn were to be accompanied by serious religious appointed by the provincial of the respective religious order. But as for Carmelites, Trinitarians, and Mercedarians (orders that were considered to be lacking the number of observants who would be able to assist the bishops in carrying out the reform of the conventuals), he obtained another brief in 1567 instructing that two Dominicans were to accompany the bishop's delegate.

This action of the king coldly ignored the privilege of religious exemption held by these orders and also the decree of the Council of Trent that entrusted their reform to the religious superiors. Moreover, the Carmelites in the general chapter of 1564 had pronounced themselves to be observants and renounced conventualism.

Perhaps because of the complaints of the superiors general, Pius V decided to remove the visitation from the hands of the bishops. He turned to another solution and put the work of reform in Spain into the hands of the generals, each being responsible for his own order. But he made a careful exception, and entrusted the reform of the Carmelites, Trinitarians, and Mercedarians to Dominican friars.

Pedro Fernández and Francisco Vargas, two Dominican friars, were named visitators for the Carmelites, the former of the communities in Castile, the latter, of the communities in Andalusia. They received powers to move religious from house to house and province to province, to assist superiors in their offices, and to depute other superiors from among either the Dominicans or Carmelites. They were entitled to perform all acts necessary for the visitation, correction, and reform of both head and members of all houses of friars and nuns.

## Spiritual Guide

John then, officially assigned to the Incarnation, began on a full scale what was to become his major ministry and also his reason for producing the classic works that he would be writing, works that would blaze with a new spiritual fire and eventually replace with bright light the dim intuitions of the standard meditation book. Ana María Gutiérrez, a nun there, gave this testimony: "By his words and his little notes, he had a gift for consoling those who conversed with him. This witness received some of the latter and also some papers about spiritual matters that she highly esteemed." These notes used by John in directing the nuns undoubtedly resembled the precise expressions of love and admonition that have come down to us as his *Sayings of Light and Love.*

May there be nothing [Lord] of worldly rhetoric in [these sayings] nor the long-winded and dry eloquence of weak and artificial human wisdom, which never pleases you. Let us speak to the heart words bathed in sweetness and love, which do indeed please you, removing obstacles and stumbling blocks from the paths of many souls who unknowingly trip and unconsciously walk in the path of error—poor souls who think they are right in what concerns the following of your beloved Son, Our Lord Jesus Christ, and becoming like him, imitating his life, actions, and virtues, and the form of his nakedness and purity of spirit. Father of mercies, come to our aid, for without you, Lord, we can do nothing.

The Lord has always revealed to mortals the treasures of his wisdom and his spirit, but now that the face of evil more and more bares itself, so does the Lord bare his treasures the more (1).

O Lord, my God, who will seek you with simple and pure love, and not find that you are all one can desire, for you show yourself first and go out to meet those who seek you (2).

Though the path is plain and smooth for people of good will, those who walk it will not travel far, and will do so only with difficulty if they do not have good feet, courage, and tenacity of spirit (3).

It is better to be burdened and in company with the strong than to be unburdened and with the weak. When you are burdened you are close to God, your strength, who abides with the afflicted. When you are relieved of the burden you are close to yourself, your own weakness; for virtue and strength of soul grow and are confirmed in the trials of patience (4).

The virtuous soul that is alone and without a master is like a lone burning coal; it will grow colder rather than hotter (7).

Those who fall alone remain alone in their fall, and they value their soul little since they entrust it to themselves alone (8).

If you do not fear falling alone, do you presume that you will rise up alone? Consider how much more can be accomplished by two together than by one alone (9).

O sweetest love of God, so little known, whoever has found its veins is at rest! (16).

God is more pleased by one work, however small, done secretly, without desire that it be known, than a thousand done with the desire that people know of them. Those who work for God with purest love not only care nothing about whether others see their works, but do not even seek that God himself know of them. Such persons would not cease to render God the same services, with the same joy and purity of love, even if God were never to know of these (20).

John carried out his mission as spiritual director at the Incarnation for five years. He guided Teresa of Jesus as well as the other nuns and was able to observe closely how the Lord communicated intimately with her. It was during this period, <u>under his direction</u>, that <u>she reached the summit of her mystical experience—the spiritual marriage</u>. During those years, John joined Teresa and her nuns in the festive custom of composing, for special occasions, devotional poems. In her letters Teresa wrote glowingly of his ministry at the Incarnation: "I believe it was Father John of the Cross who brought about all this change in the monastery." And again she wrote: "After he left I could find no one like him in all Castile."

## A Prisoner

During this time the prior general of the Carmelites residing in Rome maintained that any work to reform the friars in Spain should be carried out under his authority and diligently sought to forestall any infringement on the order's privileges. Much of the ensuing controversy between Teresa's friars and those of the observance grew out of the various interpretations that the authorities in question gave to the powers granted them by the Holy See.

Between Teresa and Fernández a deep mutual respect and an easy working relationship developed. More and more she turned to him for her permissions because she couldn't get the Carmelite provincial to answer her letters. By turning to Teresa's friars for help in reforming the Carmelite order, however, both visitators drew the friars beyond the limits established by the prior general when he allowed for a few houses of contemplative (or discalced friars). But Vargas caused the major problem by requesting three foundations of discalced friars in Andalusia, something strictly forbidden by the general, who had experienced turmoil and resistance in his visitation of the Carmelite friars there; the situation still required his close attention.

When the Carmelite order convened a chapter in Piacenza, Italy, in May 1575, no time was lost in addressing the question of discalced friars in Andalusia. The chapter reaffirmed in no uncertain terms the position the prior general had thus far taken.

Those who had been made superiors against the obedience due superiors within the order itself, or who had accepted offices or lived in monasteries or places prohibited by the same superiors, should be removed, with the aid of the secular arm if necessary. Those resisting would be considered disobedient, rebellious, and contumacious and were to be severely punished. The monasteries of discalced friars in Andalusia were to be abandoned within three days. The friars and nuns were not to go completely barefoot. Neither were they to be referred to as "discalced," but as "contemplatives" or "primitives."

In the previous August, Gregory XIII, the new pope, had declared the end of the Dominican visitation and ordained that from then on the Carmelites should be visited by the prior general and his delegates. However, what had been established by the Dominican visitators was to remain in effect. Afterward, the papal nuncio Nicolas Ormaneto received assurance that the recall of the Dominican visitators in no way affected his own powers as nuncio to visit and reform religious orders. Offended because the visitation had been called officially to a close without word to him, the king imperiously declared Gregory's papal brief to be invalid because it lacked his royal placet.

In view of the chapter of Piacenza, John realized that his presence at the Incarnation had become a cause of tension. He proposed to resign as vicar and confessor at the Incarnation, but the nuns appealed against it, and the nuncio ordered the discalced friar to remain at his post.

When Ormaneto died in June 1577, John was left at the Incarnation without support. In December of that same year, a group of Carmelites and men-at-arms broke into Fray John's quarters and spirited him away to the Carmelite monastery in Toledo. There he was secretly imprisoned as a rebel. His prison was a hole in the wall, like a closet, that had been made to serve as a lavatory in the back of a room reserved for special guests. The makeshift prison cell had no window, but only a loophole, three fingers wide, high up on the wall. Little light came through this chink. The cell measured about nine by five feet. The furniture consisted of a board on the floor with two blankets on top and a bench for the breviary, the only book allowed. No change of clothes was ever provided, and the scapular and cowl were taken away because Fray John of the Cross was a rebel. By our standards the punishment was cruel and unjust. But those who imprisoned him considered him to be "contumacious" and "rebellious." They thought that by treating him harshly they could get him to repent of his rebelliousness and submit to the commands of Piacenza. But he maintained that he had been under assignment by Ormaneto and that the apostolic visitator had the authority above that of the superiors of the order to give commands to religious. He refused to renounce the Teresian reform.

Intolerance, imprisonment, and torture were common in societies and churches before the coming of the Enlightenment, and not only in Spain or in the Catholic Church. For the most part prisons in Spain were preventive, populated by suspect criminals waiting for a sentence, like punishment by the galleys, public lashings, exile, or death. But there were many jurisdictions and they jealously guarded their privileges. Offenders in one social group had to be judged, condemned, or absolved within their own jurisdiction. Some jurisdictions were severe, others more lenient. Under the more lenient ones were the Inquisition prisons and the monastery prisons for friars and nuns of their respective orders. Less known, the monastery prisons were the more numerous, each monastery having its own, which was watched over by a member of the community who acted as a jailer. Any jailer who turned soft was subject to harsh penalties. Even the constitutions given to St. Teresa and her nuns when they gained their independence in 1581 included, by necessity, an entire detailed list of offenses and punishments in which the prison cell emerges as the destiny of those who fall into a most serious infraction. Escape from prison, even monastery prisons, was not uncommon.

For nine months John lived in obscurity and pain, physically and spiritually—the dark night par excellence. To pass the time and keep his mind active he composed poetry, some of it astonishing; for example, thirty-one stanzas of the *Spiritual Canticle*, songs of daring love. Choosing at one point to make a break for freedom rather than rot, he devised and managed to carry off a dramatic escape in the middle of the night; he took his poems with him. Finding refuge first among the discalced Carmelite nuns in Toledo, he was later provided with secret lodging in a nearby hospital through a benefactor of the nuns until his strength was restored and he was able to flee in hiding to a monastery discalced of friars.

### Free to Serve in Andalusia

For safety's sake his discalced Carmelite superiors transferred him to Andalusia, a region swelling with mountains and valleys, woods, thickets, and wildflowers full of color in the sun. Refined through suffering, immersed in a tranquil environment, he began anew his work of spiritual guidance with nuns and friars. After sharing with the nuns in Beas his *Spiritual Canticle*, he heeded their persistent requests and began commenting for them on its mystical lines.

Beginning in November 1578, John spent seven months as prior in El Calvario, a remote monastery in the deep seclusion of the mountains. From there he was sent to Baeza to organize a new house of studies for the discalced friars in Andalusia and serve as rector. Baeza was a city sparkling with enthusiasm, with many priests, friars, and nuns—and many beatas (lay women who lived in their homes and devoted themselves to the prayer of recollection). Visions, revelations, raptures, transports, a whole host of flamboyant experiences were the cherished subjects for spiritual discussion on the part of many. In this milieu Fray John of the Cross was sought after as a spiritual guide by a number of people in the town and some professors from the university. A university professor under his direction, after attending one of the intellectually disciplined academic debates led by John at the discalced house, left there saying: "What a profound man we have here! He could have held a chair in Salamanca or Alcalá de Henares."

Fray John of the Cross's guidance of the spiritual seekers in Baeza was sober.

Thus, the spiritual master should try to see to it that his disciples are not detained by the desire to pay heed to supernatural apprehensions (which are no more than small particles of spirit and the only thing the disciples will be left with), and he should turn them away from all visions and locutions and teach them to remain in freedom and the darkness of faith, in which liberty and abundance of spirit are received, and, consequently, the wisdom and understanding proper to God's words. (A 2.19.11)

As he does with his readers in the *Ascent of Mount Carmel*, he urged them to journey to God in the stark recollection of faith, a recollection that reaches beyond particular knowledge to a general loving knowledge of God. These enthusiasts thought their ecstasies, visions, and revelations were the journey's end. They tended to gauge the quality of their spiritual life by these phenomena, something they could experience and understand. John urged them to adapt in faith to the mode of God, who is simple and speaks only one Word in the contemplative simplicity and silence of faith.

God's words and visions in this and other ways may be true and certain, yet they can mislead us if we do not know how to understand them in a lofty manner and principally according to the purpose and the meaning God has in giving them. The safest and most suitable method of procedure is to oblige souls to flee prudently from these supernatural things, and to accustom them . . . to purity of spirit in dark faith—the means toward union. (A 2.19.14)

Should you tell me that everything will be all right since the first kind of illumination [locutions] is no obstacle to the second, I would reply that it is a serious obstacle if the soul pays attention to it. For this would involve attention to clear things, things of little importance and enough to hinder the communication of the abyss of faith. In this faith God supernaturally and secretly teaches the soul and raises it up in virtues and gifts in a way unknown to it. (A 2.29.7)

*then why would God*
*give them*

From time to time Fray John of the Cross would slip away from the bustle of Baeza to a secluded mountain property that had been acquired by the friars. He would lose himself there for hours on end, days and nights, in pure silence, contemplating the beauty of the infinite distances.

During his time in Baeza the tangled troubles the discalced friars were having within the order came to an end. On 22 June 1580 Gregory XIII issued a brief allowing the discalced Carmelites to exist as a separate province with their own jurisdiction and superiors. Teresa wrote, "Now we are all at peace, calced and discalced; no one can hinder us from serving our Lord."

## Called to Granada

By this time about forty years old, John, a holy man of many talents, was in demand. He undertook tiring journeys to assist the discalced Carmelite nuns, which included preparations for a foundation of theirs in Granada. At the beginning of 1582 he himself was transferred to Granada to respond there as prior to a call to remedy the community's situation.

The friars' Granada monastery was located on a desolate hill. The community was small, the living quarters confined, and the garden dried out. The view, however, was magnificent—a grand sweep of fertile plain before them; and behind them, the splendor of the Alhambra and the Sierra Nevada mountains. John could not desert a place like this in spite of the need for costly construction projects. Here was a duty that utilized all of his talents, providing posterity with a practical example of how an intense interior life can go hand in hand with the many vexatious demands the real world makes on one. He generously undertook many tasks exceptionally disagreeable, it would seem, to anyone who spoke of silence and withdrawal the way he did:

Oh, how happy is the soul, which ever experiences God resting and reposing within it! Oh, how fitting it is for it to withdraw from things, flee from business matters, and live in immense tranquility, so that it may not, even with the slightest speck of dust or noise, disturb or trouble its heart where the Beloved dwells. (F 4.15)

On the hill in Granada, dust stirred from the dry, unwatered ground and the noise of need shouted for a larger monastery. The growing community depended on a good garden for sustenance and demanded more cells and common rooms. Through the intervention of the king, the friars were able to bring water from the Alhambra to cultivate a garden. In the document giving them permission for the channeling of this water, the king states that he is giving them this alms "because of the devotion I have to the said order." John set to work at once to bring plentiful supplies of water to the friars' parched property. The aqueduct he then designed still stands today. From the resulting garden he was able to provide food not only for the community but for many of the famished poor of the area as well.

The time also had come to build on a larger scale, to embrace the inevitable nuisance of work projects in and around the monastery. The funds had to be raised from benefactors, and different classes of people had to be dealt with.

John did not merely supervise the work and expenditures. He participated directly at all levels: design, organization, and masonry work. To the construction properly speaking was added the decoration: the chapel was pointed, the sanctuary gilded, and the cloister quadrangle adorned with paintings. He also found in the work to be done a chance to invite his brother, known for a saintly simplicity, to come from Castile to help with the labor, thus providing him with employment. A future chronicler of the order, Francisco de Santa María, who had observed all this previous to entering the order himself later wrote:

> Two of his most important projects remain. The first is the aqueduct; the second, the cloister, the best to this date of all our monasteries in Spain. He united sturdiness of stone, architectural elegance, and beauty of light with a decorum, devotion, and frugality that attracted the eyes . . . because it seemed ever new. It became the model for all the other houses of the order.

Once finished, this great work brought Fray John esteem among Granada's elite.

## Old and New Christians

Who were these elite? The Old Christians (those of neither Jewish or Moslem background). In the reconquest of Granada in 1492, the Catholic Monarchs acquired a city with the highest population of their realm. Contributing to the high numbers were the refugee Moslems retreating there during the long war against them to regain the whole Granada territory in southeastern Andalusia. Yet toward 1580 the number of inhabitants was reduced by about one half. Natural disasters, like floods and earthquakes, were partly the cause. But there were other crises as well such as famines and plagues. John of the Cross's years in Granada were marked by an influx of poor people seeking alms, and by the epidemic of 1582. A decision also was made to uproot the *moriscos* (Moslems who had converted to Christianity and were thereby able to remain in Spain) crowded in the most populated urban sector. Their conspiracy and complicity with the Mediterranean Berbers and Turks were always a fear and a threat. This change in the morisco enclave was a symbol of the christianization that was taking place in the Moslem city.

This christianization required in the first place Old Christians from around Andalusia, from Castile, and other distant places in Spain. In addition, the massive baptism of the early inhabitants, who were legally converted from Islam around 1500, required another symbolic baptism, a baptism of edifices and their purposes. The christianization of places of worship was hastily begun. Gradually, the mosques took on the appearance of churches; the minarets, bell towers. At the same time monasteries of religious orders were established: the old orders right after the reconquest; and after the Council of Trent, the new and reformed orders.

St. John of the Cross then was in Granada on one of these post-Tridentine foundations, a part of the transformations that were taking place in the unfinished city. The prime mover for the foundation was Don Luis Hurtado de Mendoza, the Count of Tendilla, the governor of the Alhambra, and the commander-in-chief of the kingdom of Granada. It was he who had offered to the discalced friars their property within his jurisdiction on the hill where the Alhambra was situated.

### John's Travels and Writings

In the six years John lived at Granada he was elected prior three times and vicar provincial (superior of the entire region of Andalusia) once. That he was a poet, a mystic, and a superior did not preclude him from being seen often with his hands a mass of mud. But besides this construction work, he became involved during these years in the founding of five new monasteries of friars and three of nuns. He was obliged to undertake an extraordinary amount of travel both for these foundations and for the business of the order, walking for the shorter journeys, but riding by donkey or mule for the longer ones. It is estimated that he traveled about sixteen thousand miles during his lifetime.

In those days traveling for the enjoyment of it was out of the question. Added to the natural hazards inherent in the rough terrain and the scorching or freezing weather were the human hazards of robbery or murder perpetrated by roving bandits. Yet John could easily be carried away by natural beauty, which manifested itself in so many forms. This eased the hardships for him. He also helped himself pass the time as he traveled the dusty or muddy primitive roads by singing passages from the Psalms or the New Testament.

Without alarm or restlessness he carried out his tasks, but succeeded as well in this busiest period of his life in creating a collection of literary and mystical writings that have become classics: parts of the *Ascent of Mount Carmel* and of his commentaries on the *Spiritual Canticle*, the *Dark Night*, and the *Living Flame of Love*. Never wanting to be an academic or a professional writer, he felt an overflow of inspiration at this time and paid heed to the need and requests of the nuns, his own friars, and others for these commentaries. In them, John seized the opportunity to communicate with his readers in writing as he did in person as mystic, teacher, and ardent lover of God. Where he saw the need for instructions, he drew on his knowledge of theology, psychology, and spiritual direction.

### Interiority

The defining factor of the spirituality of sixteenth-century Spain was the passage from objective spirituality, based on vocal prayer and external works, to another vital and subjective one built on personal experience. The fundamental, Spanish mystical way was the Franciscan spirituality of recollection. This movement of interiorization appealed as well to a number of Jews (*conversos*) and Moslems (*moriscos*) who chose to convert to Christianity and remain in Spain. They did not feel at home with many of the external Christian practices, and they were drawn to those religious orders that emphasized interiority, the life of recollection.

A great classic in Jewish spirituality of the thirteenth century is the *Zohar* (*The Book of Splendor*). Scholars think it was written by Moses de León in Castile. And a great figure in Andalusia highlighting interiority in the rich Moslem culture of that same period was Ibn Arabi, whose poetry and imagery are said to have left their mark on the Spanish mystics and even Dante. It is not difficult to find similarities in these Jewish and Moslem classics to the writings of St. John of the Cross. But these similarities can also be found in the books of the Bible, in the fathers of the church, and other Christian spiritual writers. Nonetheless, would not John of the Cross have received something from that mental universe, some images and words that perdured from the Middle Ages through so many centuries, from a time in which Jews, Moslems, and Christians lived together in peace? Might not some mark from those worlds of interiority have been left? However one may respond to questions like these about sources, John with the symbols of his poetry draws the reader into his conceptual system, which has its own language and applications.

Among the twelve poems that have reached us, three are timeless masterpieces of mystical literature: *The Spiritual Canticle, The Dark Night,* and *The Living Flame of Love. The Romances* are prized for their rich biblical and theological content. "The Spring that Flows and Runs" is remarkable for its development and the lovely allure of its symbolism. John's many hours of contemplation in the still of night before the Blessed Sacrament are reflected in the words of this poem. Using the symbol of a flowing spring, he brings us with him into the intimacy of God's trinitarian life. Once he confessed in Granada: "God communicates the mystery of the Trinity to this sinner in such a way that if His Majesty did not strengthen my weakness by a special help, it would be impossible for me to live." But ordinarily the poet knows this divine life in the night of faith as hidden in the bread of life.

> *For I know well the spring that flows and runs,*
> *although it is night.*
>
> . . . . . . . . . . . . . . .
>
> 9. This eternal spring is hidden
> in this living bread for our life's sake,
> *although it is night.*
>
> 10. It is here calling out to creatures;
> and they satisfy their thirst,
> although in darkness,
> *because it is night.*
>
> 11. This living spring that I long for,
> I see in this bread of life,
> *although it is night.* (P 8)

### Final Years

In 1588 Fray John of the Cross was called back to Castile to be prior of the house in Segovia with the additional burden of reconstructing and enlarging the monastery and church as in

Granada. He was elected as well to be first councillor and pro-vicar general at a time when tensions were mounting within the government of the discalced friars themselves. In Segovia John kept alive unrelentingly his life of contemplation and solitude; community and manual labor; spiritual guidance and government. But his traveling days had come to a halt, and he wrote no more. He seemed to pass easily from the quarry to the choir and from the construction workers to silent adoration. "I often saw him leave his cell in Segovia and go up to some rocky cliffs in the garden of that monastery, and there he entered into a little cave, about the size of a man bending over, from where one could see an expanse of sky, the river, and the fields. Sometimes here, sometimes at the window of his cell looking to the sky, at other times before the Blessed Sacrament, he spent long hours in prayer," reported a member of his community.

After three effective years in Segovia, John attended a general chapter in Madrid in June 1591. The atmosphere in the chapter was strained, with gusts of emotion rising and falling. John's opinions about government of the nuns did not win the day. In some other debated points as well he ended up on the wrong side of those wielding the power. The outcome of it all was that Fray John of the Cross received a commission to go to the missions in Mexico. Although he had volunteered, more than one friar thought he was assigned to Mexico out of a desire to banish him. But he seemed untroubled by these events and wrote to one of his sympathizers:

Do not let what is happening to me, daughter, cause you any grief for it does not cause me any. . . . Think nothing else but that God ordains all, and where there is no love, put love, and you will draw out love. (L 26)

John went south again to Andalusia to the solitary monastery of La Peñuela to prepare for missionary life. At this time the rancorous Fray Diego Evangelista, a self-appointed muckraker who bore a grudge against John, his former superior, began trying to dig up damaging information against him and have him expelled from the order. Terrified by Fray Diego's harassment, the nuns in

Granada, Málaga, and Seville burned many letters and notebooks that contained encouraging words and elevating thoughts from John. Here is an excerpt from the kind of poignant letter he could write; it is addressed to a lay woman in Granada, Doña Juana de Pedraza, who was suffering from what John wrote of symbolically as a dark night:

Since you walk in these darknesses and voids of spiritual poverty, you think that everyone and everything is failing you. It is no wonder that in this it also seems that God is failing you. But nothing is failing you, neither do you have to discuss anything, nor is there anything to discuss, nor do you know this, nor will you find it, because all of these are doubts without basis. Those who desire nothing else than God walk not in darkness however poor and dark they are in their own sight. . . . You are making good progress. Do not worry, but be glad! Who are you that you should guide yourself? Wouldn't that end up fine!

You were never better off than now, because you were never so humble or so submissive, or considered yourself and all worldly things to be so small; nor did you know that you were so evil or that God was so good, nor did you serve God so purely and so disinterestedly as now, nor do you follow after the imperfections of your own will and interests as perhaps you were accustomed to do. What is it you desire? What kind of life or method of procedure do you paint for yourself in this life? What do you think serving God involves other than avoiding evil, keeping his commandments, and being occupied with the things of God as best we can? When this is had, what need is there of other apprehensions or other lights and satisfactions from this source or that. In these there is hardly ever a lack of stumbling blocks and dangers for the soul, which by its understanding and appetites is deceived and charmed; and its own faculties cause it to err. And thus God does one a great favor when he darkens the faculties and impoverishes the soul in such a way that one cannot err with these. And if one does not err in this, what need is there in order to be right other than to walk along the level road of the law of God and of the

Church, and live only in dark and true faith and certain hope and complete charity, expecting all our blessings in heaven, living here below like pilgrims, the poor, the exiled, orphans, the thirsty, without a road and without anything, hoping for everything in heaven? . . .

Should you have some problem, write to me about it. Write soon, and more frequently, for you can do so in care of Doña Ana when you are unable to do so through the nuns.

I have been somewhat ill. Now I am well, but Fray Juan Evangelista is sick. Commend him and me also to God, my daughter in the Lord.

From Segovia, October 12, 1589. (L 19)

But the dubious plans for Mexico and the sullen schemes of Diego Evangelista all came to nothing. A few months after his arrival in La Peñuela, Fray John took sick with fever and gangrenous sores. He was transferred to Ubeda for medical attention, but he did not improve. The fever increased and an abscess appeared on his thigh, spreading in a short time to the instep of his right foot. The medical treatments were excruciating and ineffective, and the humble friar sought relief in biblical passages that rose softly to his lips. After eagerly listening to the loving words of the Song of Songs, as the bell rang for Matins, he died on 14 December 1591, right after midnight. It was Saturday, Our Lady's day, and he went gently as he had lived to sing Matins in heaven. This he had predicted. The bell for Matins then shifted to a toll telling the people that Fray John of the Cross had just died. He was forty-nine. His last words were borrowed from Jesus: "Into your hands Lord, I commend my spirit."

> With flowers and emeralds
> chosen on cool mornings
> we shall weave garlands
> flowering in your love,
> and bound with one hair of mine.
>
> You considered
> that one hair fluttering at my neck;

you gazed at it upon my neck
and it captivated you;
and one of my eyes wounded you.

When you looked at me
your eyes imprinted your grace in me;
for this you loved me ardently;
and thus my eyes deserved
to adore what they beheld in you. (C 21, 22, 23)

This divine love—it was John's element, and he had longed in his lifetime to draw others to share in its delights. But even so, despite all his brilliance and artistic vision, he could not have imagined that more than four hundred years later his writings and his witness would be so powerful in attracting those who recognize him not only as an authentic guide in the spiritual life but also as a singer of true and beautiful songs.

# Chapter 2

# Leaking Cisterns

A discovery of our times is that illness, psychological and physical, can grow from a menacing fear of knowledge of self, of one's hidden emotions, impulses, and capabilities. This fear has its purpose: it protects our self-image, the love and respect we want to have for ourselves and to receive from others. It will defend these against whatever appears threatening. The mind must allow no knowledge to enter its world that could cause the feeling of being inferior, weak, or worthless. Relying on a system of ideas or powers, human beings find support in strong persons, absorbing activities, the passion of sports, the dedicated way of life. Like a soft float, these keep a person buoyed up and ignorant of self, of the truth that one is not resting in one's center. Freud summed it up with a jarring remark about life's bitter truth, stating that psychoanalysis cured the neurotic misery in order to introduce the patient to the common misery of life. No complicated technique can shake off reality, and reality is the misery.

Sometimes readers recoil from John of the Cross's *Ascent of Mount Carmel*, from his blunt picture of our human misery, our disgusting passions, appetites, and attachments, a picture we don't like to look at for long. This picture renders John's understanding of the "old self" (the usual English translation of what rendered literally would be "old man"). Like St. Paul, he sets before us the unavoidable tension and conflict existing between the "old self" and the "new self." The values of each are radically opposed.

In the following passage from the first chapter in the *Ascent*, he offers a sketch of the program that must be followed by anyone who wants to shed the gray misery of the old self and put on new, brightly colored garments offered us in Christ.

Those desiring to climb to the summit of the mount in order to become an altar for the offering of a sacrifice of pure love and praise and reverence to God must first accomplish these three tasks perfectly. First, they must cast out strange gods, all alien affections and attachments. Second, by denying these appetites and repenting of them—through the dark night of the senses—they must purify themselves of the residue. Third, in order to reach the top of this high mount, their garments must be changed. By means of the first two works, God will substitute new garments for the old. The soul will be clothed in a new understanding of God in God (through removal of the old understanding) and in a new love of God in God, once the will is stripped of all the old cravings and satisfactions. And God will vest the soul with new knowledge when the other old ideas and images are cast aside [Col. 3:9]. He causes all that is of the old self, the abilities of one's natural being, to cease and attires all the faculties with new supernatural abilities. (A 1.5.7)

Directing the reader's attention to alien affections, attachments, and appetites, John associates them with the old self; they smother the first sparks of any new life. His usual term for the cravings, satisfactions, and affections of the old self is "appetites." Just as easily, he could have used the term "sin." The old self keeps alive on sin, it thrives on sin like a rat on garbage. But John set out to teach us how to reach our purpose: union with God. Everything that could be a roadblock called out for his attention—imperfections too. So instead of "sin" he used the word "appetite," which was for him a term broad enough to include under its umbrella all that he wished, even the unrecognized imperfections you grow aware of in the dark night.

We can seriously misconstrue the teaching of the *Ascent* if we misinterpret the word "appetite." When speaking of appetites, John means willful, inordinate longings or cravings, impulses that are not rightly ordered to what is morally good or to what is beneficial for our spiritual growth. Everyone has experiences of inordinate cravings that are not willful. These are a part of the human condition and, ordinarily, do not prevent us from reaching our goal. The appetites, or cravings, then, as used by John, are willful and deformed; they need to be transformed if humans are to be liberated from their common misery.

What are the objects of the appetites? What are the things they seek? They seek good things, first of all. John classifies these objects so that he can explain and make us aware in detail of the multifaceted ways in which humans get tangled up in life's misery. The first three classes of goods belong to the more exterior spheres of our life. John names them temporal, natural, and sensory. The last three belong to the more interior, and they are the moral, supernatural, and spiritual. At this point in our reflections, it will be enough to concentrate on the first three, the more exterior. In themselves these good things are not a problem. The woe lies within the heart, or, to be precise, in the choices one makes.

### Traces of God

Everything God made is good. So before dwelling further on the havoc caused by the appetites for creatures, we can reflect on some words from John's commentary in the *Spiritual Canticle* on the goodness and beauty of creation.

> Pouring out a thousand graces,
> he passed these groves in haste;
> and having looked at them,
> with his image alone,
> clothed them in beauty.

In this stanza the creatures answer the soul. Their answer, as St. Augustine also declares . . . is the testimony that they in themselves give of God's grandeur and excellence. It is for this testimony that the soul asked in her reflections. The substance of the stanza is that God created all things with remarkable ease and brevity, and in them he left some trace of who he is, not only in giving all things being from nothing, but even by endowing them with innumerable graces and qualities, making them beautiful in a wonderful order and unfailing dependence on one another. All of this he did through his own Wisdom, the Word, his only begotten Son by whom he created them. She then says:

> Pouring out a thousand graces,

These "thousand graces" she says he was pouring out refer to the numberless multitude of creatures. She records the high number, a thousand, to indicate their multitude. She calls them graces because of the many graces he has endowed creatures with. Pouring these out, that is, stocking the whole world with them,

> He passed these groves in haste;

. . . And she says "he passed" because creatures are like a trace of God's passing. Through them one can track down his grandeur, might, wisdom, and other divine attributes. . . .

> And having looked at them,
> with his image alone,
> clothed them in beauty.

St. Paul says: "the Son of God is the splendor of his glory and the image of his substance" [Heb. 1:3]. It should be known that only with this figure, his Son, did God look at all things, that is, he communicated to them their natural being and many natural graces and gifts, and made them complete and perfect, as is said in Genesis: "God looked at all things that he made, and they were very good" [Gen. 1:31]. To look and behold that they were very good was to make them very good in the Word, his Son.

Not only by looking at them did he communicate natural being and graces, as we said, but also with this image of his Son alone, he clothed them in beauty by imparting to them supernatural being. This he did when he became man and elevated human nature in the beauty of God, and consequently all creatures, since in human nature he was united with them all. Accordingly, the Son of God proclaimed: "If I be lifted up from the earth, I will elevate all things to myself" [John 12:32]. And in this elevation of all things through the Incarnation of his Son and through the glory of his resurrection according to the flesh not only did the Father beautify creatures partially, but, we can say, he clothed them entirely in beauty and dignity. (C 5.1-4)

This latter elevation of creatures brings about an entirely new beauty to creation, but this new being only unfolds in time at a human pace, as will be explained.

If John insists that we become ugly, abject, and miserable by our love for creatures, he certainly could not be accused of Gnostic or Manichean thought, that is, that matter originated from an evil principle and that the spirit needs to be rescued from an evil material environment.

John drew his vision of the created universe as manifesting traces of the divine attributes from his reflections on sacred Scripture. Nonetheless, when human beings turn from God, the center of their lives, and choose the created world for their center, for the object of their mortal dreams, or attach themselves to it as if it were on an equal footing with God, then a desolate wind drives a gray cloud over them, and the created world loses its splendor. John has bitter descriptions for what creation is for the one who places it on a par with God.

All creatures of heaven and earth are nothing when compared to God. . . . all the being of creatures compared to the infinite being of God is nothing. . . . All the beauty of creatures compared to the infinite beauty of God is the height of ugliness. . . . All the grace and elegance of creatures compared to God's grace is utter coarseness and crudity. Compared to the infinite goodness of God, all the goodness of the creatures of the world can be called wickedness. . . . All the world's wisdom and human ability compared to the infinite wisdom of God is pure and utter ignorance. . . . All the sovereignty and freedom of the world compared to the freedom and sovereignty of the Spirit of God is utter slavery, anguish, and captivity. . . . All the delights and satisfactions of the will in the things of the world compared to all the delight that is God are intense suffering, torment, and bitterness. . . . All the wealth and glory of creation compared to the wealth that is God is utter poverty and misery.

Divine Wisdom, with pity for these souls that become ugly, abject, miserable, and poor on account of their love for worldly things, which in their opinion are rich and beautiful, exclaims in Proverbs: "O people, I cry to you, my voice is directed to the children of this earth. Be attentive, little ones, to cunning and sagacity; and you ignorant, be careful. Listen, because I want to speak of great things. Riches and glory are mine, high riches and justice. The fruit you will find in me is better than gold and precious stones; and my generations (what will be engendered of me in your souls) are better than choice silver. I walk along the ways of justice, in the midst of the paths of judgment, to enrich those who love me and to fill their treasures completely" [Prov. 8:4–6, 18–21].

Divine Wisdom speaks, here, to all those who are attached to the things of the world. She calls them little ones because they become as little as the things they love. She tells them, accordingly, to be cunning and careful, that she is dealing with great things, not small things, as they are; and that the riches and glory they love are with her and in her, not where they think; and that lofty riches and justice are present in her. Although in their opinion the things of this world are riches, she tells them to bear in mind that her riches are more precious, that the fruit found in them will be better than gold and precious stones, and that what she begets in souls has greater value than cherished silver, which signifies every kind of affection possible in this life. (A 1.4)

## The Appetites of the Old Self

These truths do not touch the outworn heart immersed in the life of the old self. Such a heart looks at the good things of the created world as though they were there for its own indulgence, all of which results in a cascade of appetites that "weary, torment, darken, defile and weaken the soul."

John divides the good things of life into different categories. In the category of temporal goods, he includes riches, status, positions, and whatever else may contribute to one's prestige, like children, relatives, marriages, and so on. Although admittedly some of his examples reflect the culture of his times, what he deals with may be found existing everywhere in one form or another. Who would deny the daily rush of energy that pours into the procurement of wealth? Who would find it odd that people work relentlessly late into the night or rise wearily before dawn to struggle for their titles and positions of prestige?

Among natural goods, John places beauty, grace, elegance, bodily constitution, and other corporeal endowments. These are the leaven of the cinema and much of the rest of the entertainment world. Finally he includes good intelligence, discretion, and the other talents belonging to the rational part of human life. These turn one's thoughts to the complex, proud world of diplomacy and academics.

The sensory goods, of course, are all those satisfying things apprehensible to the five senses of sight, hearing, smell, taste, and touch. Among these goods are also the pleasurable images of the interior power of imagination. Madison Avenue persistently teases our minds with all these delights.

Anyone engaged in the chase after these goods never has the chance to rest for long because they do not provide the appetites with a quiet place for rest. Our appetites wear us out, John says.

> . . . it is plain that the appetites are wearisome and tiring. They resemble little children, restless and hard to please, always whining to their mother for this thing or that, and never satisfied. Just as anyone who digs covetously for a treasure grows tired and exhausted, so does anyone who strives to acquire the appetites' demands become wearied and fatigued. And even if a soul does finally obtain them, it is still always weary because it is never satisfied. For, after all, one digs leaking cisterns

which cannot contain the water that slakes thirst. As Isaiah says: He is yet faint with thirst and his soul is empty [Isa. 29:8]. (A 1.6.6)

Humans, with their cravings, are like leaking cisterns, only feeling full for a time and soon needing more for their satisfaction, a pseudo-satisfaction that only increases the intensity of the cravings. Then, in the measure of the intensity, the appetites become a torment.

Just as a peasant, covetous of the desired harvest, goads and torments the ox that pulls the plow, so concupiscence, in order to attain the object of its longing, afflicts the one who lives under the yoke of the appetites. (A 1.7.1)

Next, clear thinking turns cloudy, the ability to make correct moral judgments diminishes, and a treasure of divine light is lost.

... a person's intellect clouded by the appetites, becomes dark and impedes the sun of either natural reason or God's supernatural wisdom from shining within and completely illumining it. And because of the darkening of the intellect, the will becomes weak and the memory dull and disordered in its proper operation. Since these faculties depend on the intellect in their operations, they are manifestly disordered and troubled when the intellect is hindered. . . . Oh, if people but knew what a treasure of divine light this blindness caused by their affections and appetites takes from them and the number of misfortunes and evils these appetites cause each day when left unmortified. . . . Who would have thought that a man as perfect in wisdom and gifts of God as Solomon could have sunk into such blindness and torpor of will, when he was already old, as to construct altars to countless idols and then worship them himself? (A 1.8)

In the fourth misery, the beauty of God's image turns ugly:

Inordinate appetites defile and dirty the soul, in itself a perfect and extremely beautiful image of God. (A 1.9.1)

Finally, the appetites make the practice of virtue burdensome, distasteful, and gloomy, weakening the life of virtue and even killing it.

So the unmortified appetites result in killing the soul in its relationship with God, and thus, because it [the soul] did not put them to death first, they alone live in it. . . . it is sad to see the condition of the poor soul in whom they dwell. How unhappy it is with itself, how cold toward its neighbors, how sluggish and slothful in the things of God. (A 1.10)

Thus does John end his unflattering descriptions of the hollow life of sinners: they are unhappy in themselves, unhappy with others, and unhappy with God. All dealings with the problems of life, all reactions to them, all analyses of them are conditioned through and through by the degree to which people allow the appetites to reign.

Oh, what a miserable lot this life is! We live in the midst of so much danger and find it so hard to arrive at truth. The clearest and truest things are darkest and most dubious to us and consequently we flee from what most suits us. (N 2.16.12)

In our anxiety to set the world right, to solve the persistent problems of hunger, poverty, and social injustice, all the whirling confusion in the world, we may well be adding to the confusion through obliviousness and neglect of the confusion close to home, the confusion in our own minds, caused by our cravings, which then become the mother of all other confusions.

## Misplaced Joy

Since any joy bounding up from the satisfaction of our appetites is short-lived, humans are driven to go on searching for new ways to escape sadness, more objects in which to experience the joy coming from what they possess. John has also analyzed and described the rueful results of joy, and he is referring to disordered joy.

Forgetful and sluggish about matters pertaining to their salvation, they become much more alive and astute in the things of
the world. . . . Thus in the affairs of God they are nothing, and
in those of the world they are everything. These, precisely are
the greedy. Their appetite and joy are already so extended and
dispersed among creatures—and with such anxiety—that they
cannot be satisfied. . . .The reason for this dissatisfaction is that
creatures do not slake the thirst of the avaricious, but rather
intensify it. These greedy persons fall into thousands of kinds
of sins out of love for temporal goods. . . .

Out there in the world, their reason darkened as to spiritual
matters through covetousness, they serve money and not God,
they are moved by money rather than by God, and they give
first consideration to the temporal price and not to the divine
value and reward. In countless ways they make money their
principal god and goal and give it precedence over God, their
ultimate end. . . . they do not hesitate to sacrifice their lives
when they observe that this god of theirs undergoes some temporal loss. They despair and commit suicide for wretched reasons, and demonstrate with their own hands the miserable
reward that comes from such a god. Since there is nothing to
hope for from him, he gives despair and death. And those
whom he does not pursue right up to death, the ultimate injury,
die from living in the affliction of anxieties and many other miseries. He does not permit gladness to enter their hearts or for
any earthly good to bring them joy. Insofar as they are afflicted
about money, they are always paying the tribute of their hearts
to it. . . . But even those to whom less harm comes should be
pitied greatly, since, as we affirmed, this joy causes the soul
to fall far back in the way of God. As David declares: "Do not
fear when a man becomes rich" (do not be envious, thinking
that he has an advantage over you), "for when he dies he will
take nothing with him." (A 3.19.7–11)

The list of miseries provoked by misplaced joy in the multiple
and varied objects of the senses is long, and John runs through
them quickly. They stretch from envy, gossiping, and ill-health to
disgust for the poor and lack of charity toward one's neighbor.

It can be wearisome in itself to have to read about these woes of our human condition, but the whole condition is seriously exacerbated in the culture of our times and the society in which we live. The term in vogue is "consumerism" or the "consumer society." The excited world of advertising tells people, beginning before they are able to reason, that they must have all the shining products laid before them. If they don't have them they are somehow or other inadequate, even despicable. Advertisers even interject values into their wares, suggesting that if you buy them you will be acquiring as well these very values.

John of the Cross keeps pointing out that "freedom cannot abide in a heart dominated by desires." The danger of having money and the freedom to buy and produce is that we might be enslaved not only by these objects but by the economic systems that produce them.

The vicious circle begins: the manipulated need, the promise of joy, the frustrated expectation, the guilt, and the consequent greater need to buy. Worst of all, people's merit is judged by their property.


### Feeling Alive

Carrying the problem further, we find that a self fed on its accumulations expands, gathers mass and volume like a snowball. There is no limit to our insatiable possessiveness or greed. One who needs things to fill the void is left with ever-fading memories of past feelings of self-expansion and has to keep reproducing those experiences in order to feel alive. A new property, a larger mansion will stimulate, but only for a time, the feelings of fullness and life. Moreover, people fear they might not have these things in the future. They are frightened by the unknown and long to learn everything possible about what is to come so as to ward off dangers and take advantage of opportunities.

All these human woes and a sea of others arise in the life of the old self, which is based on that experience of being alive when a craving is satisfied. Deny all your cravings and you will feel dead, for since the objects of these appetites become substitutes for God, they lead us to the margins of nothingness. Were it not for God, all these objects and we along with them would, in fact, sink into nothingness.

### God or an Idol

The greatest misery that the appetites can pour down on human beings is not any of those many that were mentioned but the desolate loss of God. To be sure, such a loss comes about in different degrees, in the measure that the appetites make a person less capable of God.

John has a key principle: love effects a likeness between the lover and the loved object. Anyone who chooses a creature in the place of God makes an idol of that creature and becomes as low as that creature and in some ways even lower because "love not only equates but even subjects the lover to the loved creature" (A 1.4.3). The subjection becomes evident when our cravings make us terrified of any hint at death to the old self whose life we have come to prize. Although it is nothing and gives only the illusion of life, we cling to that life and protect ourselves from the thought of having to lose it for God.

These evils do not unmask themselves at the moment the appetite is being satisfied, since the pleasure of the moment is an obstacle to this. Yet sooner or later the harmful effects will certainly be felt. A good illustration of this is found in the Apocalypse. An angel commanded St. John to eat the book, which was sweet to the mouth, but bitter in the stomach [Rev. 10:9]. For the appetite when satisfied seems sweet and pleasant, but eventually the bitter effect is felt. This truth will certainly be clear to those who allow themselves to be carried away by their appetites. I realize, however, that there are some so blind and unaware that they do not experience this bitter effect. Since they do not walk in God, they do not perceive what keeps them from him. (A 1.12.5)

So as to perceive these truths and be freed of all fear of self-knowledge, human beings have received an invitation to walk in God. To begin to walk in God one needs to set off into the night of faith where the life of the old self falls still.

To come to enjoy what you have not
you must go by a way in which you enjoy not.
To come to the knowledge you have not
you must go by a way in which you know not.
To come to the possession you have not
you must go by a way in which you possess not.
To come to be what you are not
you must go by a way in which you are not. (A 1.13.11)

# Chapter 3

# I Will Show My Brightness
# to the Bride

In the dark, cramped prison cell of Toledo, John of the Cross received a flash of insight for a poem about a dialogue he imagined occurring in the heart of the Holy Trinity. He expressed it in a long form named the *Romances* (P 9.1).

> In the beginning the Word
> was; he lived in God
> and possessed in him
> his infinite happiness.
> That same Word was God,
> who is the Beginning;
> he was in the beginning
> and had no beginning. . . .
> The Word is called Son;
> he was born of the Beginning. . . .
> And thus the glory of the Son
> was the Father's glory,
> and the Father possessed
> all his glory in the Son.
> As the lover in the beloved
> each lived in the other,
> and the Love that unites them
> is one with them,
> their equal, excellent as
> the One and the other:
> Three Persons, and one Beloved
> among all three. . . .

### The Father's Plan

A loving exchange takes place between Father and Son, opening a glowing path that would make possible a future loving exchange between God and his creature.

> For the being that the three possess
> each of them possesses,
> and each of them loves
> him who bears this being. . . .
> In that immense love
> proceeding from the two
> the Father spoke words
> of great affection to the Son,
>
> . . . . . . . . . . .
> "My Son, only your
> company contents me,
> and when something pleases me
> I love that thing in you;
> whoever resembles you most
> satisfies me most,
> and whoever is like you in nothing
> will find nothing in me.
> I am pleased with you alone,
> O life of my life!
> You are the light of my light,
> you are my wisdom,
> the image of my substance
> in whom I am well pleased.
> My Son, I will give myself
> to him who loves you
> and I will love him
> with the same love I have for you
> because he has loved
> you whom I love so." (P 9.1–2)

After these words of praise for his Son, the Father proceeds to describe enthusiastically the scheme of creation, all of which he plans for the pleasure of his Son and of the one who will love the Son. The God who is love does not remain enclosed and isolated but pours over into what is other than God, giving birth to creation and history.

> My Son, I wish to give you
> a bride who will love you.
> Because of you she will deserve
> to share our company,
> and eat at our table,
> the same bread I eat,
> that she may know the good
> I have in such a Son;
> and rejoice with me
> in your grace and fullness. (P 9.3)

Who is this fair bride that will be given by the Father to the Son? The bride comprises all the angels as well as all human beings, these many from two different groups becoming one bride. How can this be? Only because a flaming love for the Bridegroom will make them one. Love by its nature is outgoing, self-giving, and unitive. The yearning for God we find inscribed in human hearts is more intelligible if that yearning is rooted in God; or, that is, if God too yearns for and desires another, not out of need but out of plenitude of love.

> "I am very grateful,"
> the Son answered;
> "I will show my brightness
> to the bride you give me,
> so that by it she may see
> how great my Father is,
> . . . I will hold her in my arms
> and she will burn with your love,
> . . ."Let it be done, then," said the Father,
> for your love has deserved it.
> And by these words
> the world was created,
> a palace for the bride

made with great wisdom
and divided into rooms,
one above, the other below.
The lower was furnished
with infinite variety,
while the higher was made beautiful
with marvelous jewels,
that the bride might know
the Bridegroom she had.
The orders of angels
were placed in the higher,
but humanity was given
the lower place,
for it was in its being,
a lesser thing.
And though beings and places
were divided in this way,
yet all form one,
who is called the bride;
for love of the same Bridegroom
made one bride of them. (P 9.4)

Revealing his novel view of the created universe, a palace for the bride, John points up the high worth of human beings who have the whole material world as a palace for themselves and their Bridegroom. The truth about both God and ourselves is that we were meant to exist as persons in communion in a common household, living as persons from and for others, not in isolation or self-centeredness. All of this comes to us as gift, including our own being.

In the material world only human beings can know that creation is God's free gift, an overflow of love in which the persons of the Trinity are revealed as being for us. Although humanity must be content with the lower place, still, in the divine plan, humanity will be exalted by the Bridegroom because of the law of perfect love, which urges the lover to become like the beloved. In fact, the greater the likeness the greater the delight.

Those higher ones possessed
the Bridegroom in gladness;
the lower in hope, founded
on the faith that he infused in them,
telling them that one day
he would exalt them,
and that he would lift them
up from their lowness
so that no one
could mock it any more;
for he would make himself
wholly like them,
and he would come to them
and dwell with them;
and God would be man
and man would be God,
and he would walk with them
and eat and drink with them,
and he himself would be
with them continually
until the consummation
of this world,
when, joined, they would rejoice
in eternal song. (P 9.4)

The bride through the Love the Son will give her will enter
and share the same intimacy between the Father and the Son
with which the *Romance* opened.

[telling them] He would take her
tenderly in his arms
and there give her his love;
and when they were thus one,
he would lift her to the Father
where God's very joy
would be her joy.
For as the Father and the Son
and he who proceeds from them

> live in one another,
> so it would be with the bride;
> for, taken wholly into God,
> she will live the life of God. (P 9.4)

Hopelessly absorbed in themselves, human beings have to hear this good news of God's plan for them and freely accept to share in the Father's love of the Son. They don't seem able to help themselves in their selfishness, corrupted as they were under the tree, with their appetites set on satisfying their own desires, living the life of the old self. John finds in some words from Ezekiel the magnanimity of God's love for human beings despite their blind and bitter deeds: "You were cast out upon the earth in contempt of your soul on the day you were born. . . . And I passed by you and looked at you. . . . And I pledged myself to you and entered into a covenant with you and made you mine" (C 23.6).

If your mother, therefore, brought you death under the tree, I brought you life under the tree of the cross. . . . The Bridegroom himself literally speaks this stanza to the bride in the Song of Songs: "Under the apple tree I raised you up; there your mother was corrupted, there she who bore you was violated" [Song 8.5]. (C 23.5)

Again speaking to the Father in the *Romances,* with heart of fire, the Son exclaims:

> I will go and tell the world,
> spreading the word
> of your beauty and sweetness
> and of your sovereignty.
> I will go seek my bride
> and take upon myself
> her weariness and labors
> in which she suffers so;
> and that she may have life,
> I will die for her,
> and lifting her out of that deep,
> I will restore her to you. (P 9.7)

With each person living in the other through love, we can say that love is the life of the Trinity. Through his death of love, Christ lifts his bride up, attracts her to himself, to her destiny as bride of the Bridegroom, to share in that very saving life of the Holy Trinity.

No wrathful God, demanding punishment, or penal substitution from his Son, takes hold of John's thought. Like a shepherd boy, with heart aching for his beloved shepherdess, God bends down to the earth to raise humanity to God's realm. "And I, if I be lifted up, shall draw all things to me."

> A lone young shepherd lived in pain
> withdrawn from pleasure and contentment,
> his thoughts fixed on a shepherd-girl
> *his heart an open wound of love.*
>
> He weeps, but not from the wound of love,
> there is no pain in such affliction
> even though the heart is pierced;
> he weeps in knowing he's been forgotten.
>
> That one thought: his shining one
> has forgotten him, is such great pain
> that he bows to brutal handling in a foreign land,
> *his heart an open wound with love.*
>
> The shepherd says: I pity the one
> who draws herself back from my love,
> and does not seek the joy of my presence,
> *though my heart is an open wound with love for her.*
>
> After a long time he climbed a tree,
> and spread his shining arms,
> and hung by them, and died,
> *his heart an open wound with love.* (P 7)

The covenant, the espousal with Christ, is bestowed immediately in baptism when God gives this grace, but the espousal is not immediately perfect in the baptized. The spiritual betrothal and marriage John describes in his writings only come about gradually at a human pace (C 23.6). It is sinners who are called to this marriage, people in an unhappy state, living in a prison cell, as was John in Toledo:

The soul uses as a metaphor the wretched state of captivity. It is a sheer grace to be released from this prison without hindrance from the jailers. The soul through original sin is a captive in the mortal body, subject to passions and natural appetites; when liberated from this bondage and submission, it considers its escape, in which it is unnoticed, unimpeded, and unapprehended by its passions and appetites, a sheer grace. (A 1.15.1)

### The Soul

It would seem from the above passage that John agrees with philosophers like Plato and later Descartes, who conceived the soul as an immaterial entity having being in its own right. It would not be out of place here to examine John's understanding of the human being. Socrates, in the *Phaedo,* describes the body as the soul's prison house, or worse, the source of the soul's contamination by the impurities of sense and passion.

When John speaks of the soul, he is speaking generally in broad fashion of a human subject capable of God, the subject who suffers the dark night and reaches divine union. In speaking of the soul in relation to the body, John does not always take pains to wear the philosopher's hat. When he does, it is clear that for him the soul is not a distinct entity related to the body as a part to the whole. Although a theory of the soul that views it as having a being independent of the body would seem to harmonize more readily with his belief in the human soul's special creation, John follows the tradition of St. Thomas Aquinas, who rejects such a theory. The human being is not two beings but one; nor a soul using a body but a single entity of composite nature.

The doctrine of body and soul that holds them to be related as matter and form preserves the unity of the human being and, in the opinion of Aquinas, fits the way in which we learn through our senses, experiences, passions, and, in thinking, depend on imagination. Thus, for the present it should be enough to say that for John the soul and body form a "unity in one *suppositum*" (C 13.4). A *suppositum* is a being that has existence in itself and underlies a rational or infrarational nature. As understood in John's time, a person is a *suppositum* of a rational nature, a distinct identity. In this sense a person is nobody else.

### The Old and New Self

However, each one is an intelligible unity in an ongoing process. Nowadays we hear educators urging people to become their true selves, or pointing out that one becomes a person in one's dealings with others. What does John mean, then, when he says, following St. Paul, that the old self must die? Must you change your identity?

Since we are continually in the process of growing (in our understanding of reality, for example), it is reasonable to think that there can be a process of change without need for a change of identity. St. Paul speaks of "when I was a child." Once grown, we can all say, "I am no longer a child, a youth, a young adult, but I am still the same that I was from the beginning. After I develop more skills and habits, which all become a further phase of what I call myself, I am still the one who was from the beginning."

John speaks of the old self as living in darkness and the new self as living in light. He hardly means that we are dealing with two distinct identities. The images of light and darkness can serve as helpful illustrations. The moon with its many phases could be used as an example. In the sliver of moon we see the first glimmer of light over an otherwise dark surface. While the moon is rounding to the full, the darkness lessens until finally the entire surface of the moon is fully illuminated, suffused with light according to the capacity of its size.

John of the Cross uses the example of a crystal illuminated not only on its surface but in its depths until, illumined to its full capacity, it shines so brilliantly as to be undistinguishable from the light. Like the moon, the crystal goes through its phases from being in total darkness to being totally illumined. Appearing different in their phases, they remain the same, moon or crystal, with the capacity to be fully illuminated.

Speaking of the divine union as a total illumination of an object so that it seems to be transformed into the light, John of the Cross offers this image when explaining his notion of the nature of transformation in God.

Here is an example that will provide a better understanding of this explanation. A ray of sunlight shining on a smudgy window is unable to illumine that window completely and transform it into its own light. It could do this if the window were cleaned and polished. The less the film and stain are wiped away, the less the window will be illumined; and the cleaner the window is, the brighter will be its illumination. . . . If the window is totally clean and pure, the sunlight will so transform and illumine it that to all appearances the window will be identical with the ray of sunlight and shine just as the sun's ray. Although obviously the nature of the window is distinct from that of the sun's ray (even if the two seem identical), we can assert that the window is the ray or light of the sun by participation. The soul on which the divine light of God's being is ever shining, or better, in which it is ever dwelling by nature, is like this window, as we have affirmed.

A soul makes room for God by wiping away all the smudges and smears of creatures, by uniting its will perfectly to God's; for to love is to labor to divest and deprive oneself for God of all that is not God. When this is done the soul will be illumined by and transformed in God. And God will so communicate his supernatural being to it that it will appear to be God himself and will possess what God himself possesses. . . . and the soul appears to be God more than a soul. Indeed, it is God by participation. Yet truly, its being (even though transformed) is naturally as distinct from God's as it was before, just as the window, although illumined by the ray, has being distinct from the ray's. (A 2.5.6–7)

Christ brings the intimate life of the Trinity into our lonely darkness, a life of loving communion, a light powerful enough to expel the darkness that appeared as light and the life that was really death.

Let it be known that what the soul calls death is all that goes to make up the old self: the entire engagement of the faculties (memory, intellect, and will) in the things of the world, and the indulgence of the appetites in the pleasures of creatures. All this is the activity of the old life, which is the death of the new spiritual life. The soul is unable to live perfectly in the new life if the old self does not die completely. The Apostle warns: "Take off the old self and put on the new self who according to God is created in justice and holiness" [Eph 4:22–24]. (F 2.33)

Clearly, then, the old self that dies is not to be equated with the center of consciousness and freedom, but a mode of being in which I order all the objects I encounter according to the pattern of my private project. Other persons also I paint as objects that must submit to me and all that gives me the feeling of life. A mode of being in the world in which I order everything to my own satisfaction makes for a deformed, disordered, death-inducing existence; a deadly distortion pervades all my relationships. Such is the life of the old self: not only a form of hatred of others but a form of self-hatred as well, a life of darkness worthy of our contempt, a long distance from true personal life.

Creating the human being in his image, as bride for his Son, God inserted in all of us the tendency by nature to pour over into active self-manifestation and self-communication to others. This is done through intellect and will working together. If a person is a good person, that is, rightly ordered in conscious free action, then this active presence to others will take the form of willing what is truly good for them, which is itself a definition of love in its broadest meaning. A human person, though a distinct identity, is not an isolated, self-sufficient individual, but one whose whole being is toward friendship, community, and society, toward others in self-communicative expression.

The movement away from the old self outward toward others is the beginning of transcendence and readiness to receive the Light that has come into the world to remove our sins, our darkness. As persons we open ourselves as well to God's self-communication in Christ, the Word spoken into the world by God. When entirely permeated by Christ's life, like the moon that is full after having waxed from total darkness through its phases, Christians reach their destiny, their capacity for fullness in the complete gift of self.

## Sense and Spirit

John of the Cross views the activities of a person from the two basic fields in which human beings operate: the world of the sense and the world of the spirit. Into these areas the new life or activity must be inserted. Of course, he accepts that human beings are endowed with the power of sense and perceive through their senses. He also takes as a matter of fact the existence of the sensible—of an external something that causes sensation and can be sensed. For John human beings also have the power of spirit by which they apprehend immaterial or spiritual realities. In these two areas of sense and spirit, a process of purification must upset the deep heart's core, a transformation by fire must give shape to the new self fully lived by Christ. The new other-centered life expels the old self-centered life.

In his poem *The Dark Night*, John calls the process a night even though it imparts light, because in night, metaphorically, there is a privation, a privation of light. To attain union with the Beloved the lover must go out at night.

To understand this departure one should know that a soul must ordinarily pass through two principal kinds of night—which spiritual persons call purgations or purifications of the soul—in order to reach the state of perfection. Here we will term these purgations nights because in both of them the soul journeys in darkness as though by night.

The first night or purgation . . . concerns the sensory part of the soul. The second night . . . concerns the spiritual part. We will deal with this second night, insofar as it is active, in the second and third sections of the book. In the fourth section we will discuss the night insofar as it is passive. (A 1.1.1–2)

With respect to the passive night, John explains further.

This first night is the lot of beginners, at the time God commences to introduce them into the state of contemplation. It is a night in which their spirit also participates, as we will explain in due time. The second night or purification takes place in those who are already proficients, at the time God desires to lead them into the state of divine union. This purgation, of course, is more obscure, dark, and dreadful, as we will subsequently point out. (A 1.1–3)

With active nights comprising what humans can do themselves to break free from the ways of the old self, and passive nights comprising those privations that happen without one's inducing them, the entire person undergoes the purification whether it be of sense or spirit. But predominantly the purification will work either on sense or spirit. As will become clear, it is the life of Christ, the life of faith, hope, and love, not the privation in itself, that effects the change, as the Christian is divinized through the Holy Spirit.

### Climbing the Path in Search of the Beloved

Entitling his book about the active purification *The Ascent of Mount Carmel*, John envisioned the process also as a climb up a mountain. He drew a sketch of this mountain, which he called the "mount of perfection," in the center of which lies the path of the perfect spirit; along this path he wrote the word *nada* (nothing) seven times. On both sides of this path he listed the many things that from earth or heaven one can cling to. Among the many other items appearing in the sketch and having to do with John's vision of the journey leading to union with God, you begin to notice, on looking carefully, that actually the summit of the mount appears in the center of the drawing. Thus, the climb upward becomes also a journey inward to our center who is God. Either way the movement is in a direction opposite self-centered living.

The path of nothing would amount to just that were it not for its undergirding or, better, for what makes it the special path that it is, one leading to union with God—the path of the theological virtues. The theological virtues require all that is needed for us to be genuine disciples of Christ, who is himself this way of nothing and who revealed it to us by his life and teaching.

The first stanza of the *Spiritual Canticle* begins with a shepherd girl in love with the dream of her heart, with a shy shepherd boy, searching for him through wooded lands, mountains, and hollows. The shepherdess represents the bride-soul, and the shepherd the Bridegroom Christ. In this love song the lovers find and lose and seek again, experiencing the mournful pain of separations and the fiery delights of encounter, both absences and presences of the beloved. In beginning his commentary on the work, John sums up the detailed teaching he offers in the *Ascent* on the purifications necessary for union with God.

That this thirsting soul might find her Bridegroom and be united with him in this life through union of love insofar as possible, that she might slake her thirst with the drop of him that is receivable in this life, it would be well for us to answer for her Bridegroom, since she asks him, and point out the place where he is most surely hidden. She may then surely find him there with the perfection and delight possible in this life, and thus not wander in vain after the footprints of her companions [Song 1:7].

It should be known that the Word, the Son of God, together with the Father and the Holy Spirit, is hidden by his essence and his presence in the innermost being of the soul. Individuals who want to find him should leave all things through affection and will, enter within themselves in deepest recollection, and let all things be as though not. St. Augustine, addressing God in the *Soliloquies,* said: *I did not find you without, Lord, because I wrongly sought you without, who were within. . . .*

Oh, then, soul, most beautiful among all creatures, so anxious to know the dwelling place of your Beloved that you may go in search of him and be united with him, now we are telling you that you yourself are his dwelling and his secret inner room and hiding place. There is reason for you to be elated and joyful in seeing that all your good and hope is so close as to be within you, or better, that you cannot be without him. *Behold,* exclaims the Bridegroom, *the kingdom of God is within you* [Luke 17:21]. And his servant, the apostle St. Paul, declares: *You are the temple of God* [2 Cor. 6:16]. . . .

You do very well, O soul, to seek him ever as one hidden, for you exalt God and approach very near him when you consider him higher and deeper than anything you can reach. Hence, pay no attention, neither partially nor entirely, to anything your faculties can grasp. I mean that you should never seek satisfaction in what you understand about God, but in what you do not understand about him. Never stop with loving and delighting in your understanding and experience of God, but love and delight in what you cannot understand or experience of him. Such is the way, as we said, of seeking him in faith. However, surely it may seem that you find, experience, and understand God, you must, because he is inaccessible and concealed, always regard him as hidden, and serve him who is hidden in a secret way. Do not be like the many foolish ones who, in their lowly understanding of God, think that when they do not understand, taste, or experience him, he is far away and utterly concealed. The contrary belief would be truer. The less distinct is their understanding of him, the closer they approach him, since in the words of the prophet Daniel, he made darkness his hiding place [Ps. 18:11]. Thus in drawing near him, you will experience darkness because of the weakness of your eye.

You do well, then, at all times, in both adversity and prosperity, whether spiritual or temporal, to consider God as hidden. (C. 1.6, 7)

# Chapter 4

# The Way Out of Darkness

Christ is our way out of darkness into light. A passage from
Hebrews summoned John of the Cross's attention and pressed its
way to a central position in his teaching: "That which God formerly spoke to our fathers through the prophets in many ways
and manners, now, finally, in these days he has spoken to us all
at once in his Son" (Heb. 1:1–2).

Fasten your eyes on him alone because in him I have spoken
and revealed all and in him you will discover even more than
you ask for and desire.... For he is my entire locution and
response, vision and revelation, which I have already spoken,
answered, manifested, and revealed to you by giving him to
you as a brother, companion, master, ransom, and reward. On
that day when I descended on him with my Spirit on Mount
Tabor proclaiming:... "This is my beloved Son in whom I am
well pleased, hear him" [Matt. 17:5], I gave up these methods
of answering and teaching and presented them to him. Hear
him because I have no more faith to reveal or truths to manifest. If I spoke before, it was to promise Christ. If they questioned me, their inquiries were related to their petitions and
longings for Christ in whom they were to obtain every good,
as is now explained in all the doctrine of the evangelists and
apostles. Behold him well, for in him you will uncover all of
these [visions and revelations] already made and given, and
many more.

If you desire me to answer with a word of comfort, behold
my Son subject to me and to others out of love for me, and

afflicted, and you will see how much he answers you. If you desire me to declare some secret truths or events to you, fix your eyes only on him and you will discern hidden in him the most secret mysteries, and wisdom, and wonders of God, as my Apostle proclaims: "In the Son of God are hidden all the treasures of the wisdom and knowledge of God" [Col. 2:3]. These treasures of wisdom and knowledge will be for you far more sublime, delightful, and advantageous than what you want to know. The Apostle, therefore, gloried, affirming that he had acted as though he knew no other than Jesus Christ and him crucified [1 Cor. 2:2]. . . . behold him, become human, and you will find more than you imagine. For the Apostle also says: "In Christ all the fullness of the divinity dwells bodily" [Col. 2:9]. (A 2.22.5–6)

Taking the role of the Father, expanding on those words spoken at Our Lord's baptism and at his transfiguration as recorded in the Gospels, John urges us to behold Christ, listen to him, and consider him carefully as our teacher, companion, savior, and reward, to which we may add, from the thoughts presented in the previous chapter, friend, beloved, and Bridegroom. If, as mentioned, we must break free from the old self and seek the beloved, who remains always the hidden one, John gives us two comforting truths for our encouragement. The first is in the *Living Flame of Love*: "if anyone is seeking God, the Beloved is seeking that person much more" (3.28). The second appears in the *Spiritual Canticle*: "Great was the desire of the Bridegroom to free and ransom his bride completely from the hands of sensuality and the devil" (22.1).

John calls the person "sensual" who is held firmly in the grasp of sensuality. This mode of speaking about the contrasts in human beings reveals its roots in St. Paul:

The second spiritual benefit people procure from not desiring joy in sensible things is excellent; we can truthfully say that from sensual they become spiritual, and from animal, rational, and even that from what is human in them they advance to the angelic, and from earthly and human they become heavenly and divine. Since human beings who look for gratification and enjoyments in sensible objects deserve no other title than these we mentioned (sensual, animal, earthly, and so on), they deserve all those other titles (spiritual, heavenly, and so on), when they elevate their joy above these sensible goods. (A 3.26.3)

Noting that the old self is called the sensual self, we needn't conclude that this is because it is carrying the weight of matter or that sense puts us in direct contact with earthly things; nor does the term refer to only a part of the human composite. In John's scheme the sensual self applies to the whole person, meaning that the sensual self manifests a mode of being and acting dominated by impulses and energies focused on the life of the senses, a life in which these powers stand out boldly.

The senses belong to the sensory part of the soul, also called the lower part. This part consists of the exterior senses (hearing, sight, smell, taste, and touch) and the interior senses (mainly, imagination and fantasy). These interior sense faculties present the objects perceived through the senses, objects that stir the sensory appetites.

Those who are not so spiritual as to be purged of appetites and satisfactions, but still keep in themselves something of the animal self, believe that things most vile and base to the spirit (those closest to the senses, according to which they are still living) are highly important; and those that are loftier and more precious to the spirit (those further withdrawn from the senses), are considered to be of little value and are not esteemed by them. They will even regard them sometimes as foolishness, as St. Paul clearly indicates: "The animal self does not perceive the things of God; they are foolishness to it and it cannot understand them" [1 Cor. 2:14]. (F 3.74)

## Meditation

Becoming a disciple of Christ ordinarily must begin with the sensual self, a whole mode of being that needs to be changed. And what must be done? Sinners have grown to be good men, and good men have grown to be sinners again, and love lost as soon as won. Fasten your eyes on Christ, John says, keep turning to look on him, consider him, hear him.

Meditation is one of the spiritual exercises long associated with Christian discipleship. Meditation is a reflective prayer that awakens love of God and neighbor and prepares the disciple for the gift of contemplation. For John, meditation is a work of the senses, and contemplation a work of the spirit. In his *Sayings of Light and Love,* he repeats some words that grew out of medieval monasticism: "Seek in reading and you will find in meditation; knock in prayer and it will be opened to you in contemplation" (168). Reading and meditation. Observe Christ, listen to his words, seek to understand, ponder what they mean for me, respond to them; and let all of this enkindle love. This is how the grace of discipleship can first come to us.

From biblical times through the monastic literature and the fathers of the church to the spiritual writers of the Middle Ages, the concept of meditation saw both continuity and change. The change unfolded as the intellectual or reflective factor increased. Because Christian meditators turned to the Bible for inspiration, continuity held fast. In its primitive sense meditation meant to murmur in a low, indistinct voice. When the Hebrew word was translated into Greek and Latin, it took on further connotations of "watching over," "taking to heart," "practicing." Among the monastic writers, the first characteristic of Christian meditation was the repetition of the word of God for the sake of nourishing the soul. So the early monks would repeat in a low voice verses of the Psalms or short biblical texts, but as more monks began to engage in studies the intellectual element of meditation took over piecemeal a greater role.

The Carthusian Guigo II (twelfth century) distinguished what became the four classic degrees of meditation: reading, meditation, prayer, contemplation. Explaining meditation, he teaches that by taking the gifts offered in reading, meditation seeks to penetrate to the interior, going beyond the rind to the soft core, pith, or essential part. But by the fifteenth century the meditation procedure had gotten more detailed and complicated, inducing John Mombaer to set up a system containing some twenty-two steps. St. Ignatius of Loyola later greatly simplified Mombaer's use of the three faculties of memory, intellect, and will, and also introduced a decided use of the imagination.

Although John of the Cross's principal concern was to explain and defend the transition from meditation to contemplation, as will be seen, he elucidates in the process an important teaching on meditation. One can detect the presence of Guigo and Ignatius in his explanations of meditation.

We are speaking of two interior bodily senses: the imagination and the phantasy. They are of service to each other in due order because the one is discursive with the images and the other forms them. For our discussion there will be no need of differentiating between them. This should be remembered if we do not mention them both explicitly. All that these senses, then, can receive and construct are termed imaginations and phantasms. These are forms represented to the interior senses through material images and figures....

The natural [imaginations] are those the soul can actively construct by its own power through forms, figures, and images.

Meditation is the work of these two faculties since it is a discursive act built on forms, figures, and images, imagined and fashioned by these senses. For example: the imagining of Christ crucified or at the pillar or in some other scene; or of God seated on a throne with resplendent majesty; or the imagining and considering of glory as a beautiful light, and so on; or, in similar fashion, of any other human or divine object imaginable. (A 2.12.3–4)

To these two sense faculties John adds, in other places, a sense memory as belonging to the interior sense faculties. The sense memory serves as an archive for the objects of hearing, sight, touch, smell, and taste.

This interior sense, the phantasy, together with the memory, is for the intellect the archives or receptacle in which all the intelligible forms and images are received. Like a mirror, this faculty contains them within itself.... It in turn presents them to the intellect, and there the intellect considers and makes a judgment about them. Not only is the phantasy capable of this, but it can even compose and imagine other objects resembling those known. (A 2.16.2)

Memory and imagination require bodily organs and have the brain as the organic seat of their functioning. In this respect, scientific research continues to make new, compelling, and startling discoveries about the brain and its multifaceted activities. Not requiring physical presence to the senses like the object perceived, the object imagined need not be located in the past as is so of the object remembered, nor for that matter need it have any definite location in time and space. As the object of memory is an event that no longer exists, so the object of imagination may be something that has never existed and never will.

In describing meditation John follows a line of thought that goes back through Aquinas to Aristotle. Aristotle held that rational thought, which for him is quite distinct from imagination, cannot exist apart from imagination, the soul never thinking without an image. To understand actually, the intellect needs the act of imagination.

Aristotle's theory that the operations of thinking are always dependent on (though not reducible to) acts of imagination, does not imply that imagination is always accompanied by abstract or rational thought; sometimes imagination may be active without judgment or reasoning, as will be seen later in initial contemplation.

John always treats of meditation as "discursive," which he took to refer to movement of the thought processes from point to point. The word "discursive" has its roots in the Latin word for run about, and John uses the Spanish word *discurren* when speaking in the *Canticle* of young maidens running along the way.

### The Rind and the Substance

Caught up in the activities and emotions of the senses, those who live the life of the sensual self must be touched by grace in that place where they live, in the whirling world of the senses, which is why John views discursive meditation, a work of the senses, as a task suited to beginners. The task must lead to rest in the fruit.

Ordinarily, as often as individuals receive some profitable grace, they experience—at least spiritually—gratification in the means through which the grace is obtained. If this is not received, there will rarely be profit; neither will they find in the cause of that former gratification the support and satisfaction they did before when they received grace through that means. This agrees with what the philosophers hold: "What is savory nourishes and fattens." Hence holy Job asks: "Could one perchance eat the unsavory that is not seasoned with salt?" [Job 6:6]. . . .

It should be known that the purpose of discursive meditation on divine subjects is the acquisition of some knowledge and love of God. Each time individuals procure through meditation some of this knowledge and love they do so by an act. Many acts, in no matter what area, will engender a habit. Similarly, through many particular acts of this loving knowledge a person reaches the point in which a habit is formed in the soul. God, too, is wont to effect this habit in many souls, placing them in contemplation, without these acts as means, or at least without many of them.

What the soul, therefore, was gradually acquiring through the labor of meditation on particular ideas has now, as we said, been converted into the habitual and substantial, general, loving knowledge. This knowledge is neither distinct nor particular, as the previous. Accordingly the moment prayer begins, the soul, as one with a store of water, drinks peaceably without the labor and the need of fetching the water through the channels of past considerations, forms, and figures. . . .

This is why people experience difficulty and displeasure when, despite their being in this calm, they meet others who want to make them meditate and work with particular concepts. Their experience resembles that of the suckling child. It finds that the breast is taken away just when it is beginning to taste the milk that was gathered there for it. As a result it is forced to renew its efforts of grasping and squeezing. Or their experience is like that of a person who, while enjoying the substance of the fruit, once the rind is peeled, is forced to stop and begin again to remove the rind from the fruit even though the fruit has already been peeled. In such an instance the person would fail to find the rind and cease enjoying the substance of the fruit that is at hand. Or this is like turning away from the captured prey to go hunting for another.

Many behave similarly at the beginning of this state. They think that the whole matter consists in understanding particular ideas and in reasoning through images and forms (the rind of the spirit). Since they do not encounter these images in that loving, substantial quietude, where nothing is understood particularly and in which they like to rest, they believe they are wasting time and straying from the right road; and they turn back to search for the rind of images and reasoning. They are unsuccessful in their search because the rind has already been removed. There is no enjoyment of the substance nor ability to meditate, and they become disturbed with the thought of backsliding and going astray. Indeed they are getting lost, but not in the way they imagine, for they are losing the exercise of their own senses and first mode of experience. This loss indicates that they are approaching the spirit being imparted to them, in which the less they understand the further they penetrate into the night of the spirit—the subject of this book. They must pass through this night to a union with God beyond all knowing.

There is little to be said about the second sign, for it is obvious that these persons at this time necessarily find worldly images dissatisfying. Even those that concern God, which are more conformable to their state, fail to satisfy them, as we explained. Nevertheless, as we mentioned above, the imagination usually wanders back and forth during this recollection. But these individuals do not desire or find delight in this; rather, they are troubled about it on account of the disturbance it brings to that gratifying peace.

Nor do I believe it is necessary to indicate here why the

third sign (the loving, general knowledge or awareness of God) is a requirement for discontinuing meditation. . . .

Were individuals not to have this knowledge or attentiveness to God, they would, as a consequence, be neither doing anything nor receiving anything. Having left the discursive meditation of the sensitive faculties and still lacking contemplation (the general knowledge in which the spiritual faculties—memory, intellect, and will—are actuated and united in this passive, prepared knowledge), they would have no activity whatsoever relative to God. For a person can neither conceive nor receive knowledge already prepared save through either the sensitive or spiritual faculties. With the sensory faculties, as we affirmed, one can make discursive meditation, seek out and form knowledge from the objects; and with the spiritual faculties one can enjoy the knowledge received without any further activity of the senses. (A 2.14.2–6)

The religious images in this process of acquiring some knowledge and love of God are important because the troublesome senses of the beginner are so immersed in the activities surrounding their attachments to the world of the senses.

By these sensitive means beginners dispose their spirit and habituate it to spiritual things, and at the same time they void their senses of all other base, temporal, secular, and natural forms and images. (A 2.13.1)

The spiritual wisdom (loving knowledge) of contemplation is incomprehensible to the senses. God would begin at once to bestow it

if the two extremes (human and divine, sense and spirit) could through the ordinary process be united by only one act, and if he could exclude the many preparatory acts that are so connected in gentle and orderly fashion that, as is the case with natural agents, each is the foundation and preparation for the next. . . . Therefore God perfects people gradually, according to their human nature, and proceeds from the lowest and most exterior to the highest and most interior. . . . the interior bodily senses with which we are dealing, such as the imagination and phantasy, are gradually perfected and accustomed to good through considerations, meditations, and holy reasonings; and through all this the spirit is instructed. . . . By this method, then, God instructs people and makes them spiritual. He begins by communicating spirituality to them, in accord with their littleness or small capacity, through elements that are exterior, palpable, and accommodated to sense. He does this so that by means of the rind of those sensible things, in themselves good, the spirit, making progress in particular acts and receiving morsels of spiritual communication, may form a habit in spiritual things and reach the actual substance of spirit foreign to all sense. (A 2.17.3-5)

### The Fruit of Meditation

The loving knowledge gained from this use of the senses in meditation centers chiefly on the person of Christ, is relational and becomes a habit so that one knows him in the way one would know a friend. The Word became visible and perceptible to our senses to draw us to the invisible realities of the divine mystery. Love for the beloved Christ is the stimulus toward disentangling oneself from the appetites that contradict his presence in one's life. The whole world, with its storm and strife, in which the soul was centered before its conversion to the following of Christ, is a master that must be renounced.

Aware of the Bridegroom's words in the Gospel, that no one can serve two masters but must necessarily fail one [Matt. 6.24], the soul claims here that in order not to fail God she failed all that is not God, that is, herself and all other creatures, losing all these for love of him. (C 29.10)

This love poured into the heart through grace gives these two desires: the desire to be like Christ and the desire to serve him. The desire to be like Christ does not require a clumsy contriving at an exact reproduction, which would be impossible anyway because of our lack of historical details. For John, to become like Christ is to live in his spirit and seek no gratification other than "the fulfillment of his Father's will, which he called his meat and food" (John. 4:34).

Seeking the Father's will means making use of all one has for the honor and glory of God. This is the cardinal principle that John lays down for the reform of one's life and the service of God. The disciple's activity through the love of Christ must transcend the self (and the self's honor and glory) and move undauntedly toward another center, toward God, the authentic center, and toward God's honor and glory. We were created for the purpose of glorifying God. Words spoken in set patterns of praise glorify God. Praising God is not, however, accomplished only in the assembly or in preset patterns of prayer. In the New Testament, followers of Christ are enjoined to give glory to God not only in prayer but with their whole lives. There is the injunction in 1 Cor. 10:31 that "whether you eat or drink, or whatever you do, do everything for the glory of God."

I have found no more appropriate passage than the one in chapter 6 of Deuteronomy, where Moses commands: *You shall love the Lord, your God, with all your heart, and with all your soul, and with all your strength* [Deut. 6:5]. This passage contains all that spiritual persons must do and all that I must teach them here if they are to reach God by union of the will through charity. In it human beings receive the command to employ all the faculties, appetites, operations, and emotions of their soul in God so that they will use all this ability and strength for nothing else.... There are four of these emotions or passions: joy, hope, sorrow, and fear. These passions manifestly keep the strength and ability of the soul for God, and direct it toward him, when they are so ruled that a person rejoices only in what is purely for God's honor and glory. (A 3.16.1–2)

John of the Cross habitually carried the Bible; he dwelt in the Sacred Scriptures, reading, analyzing, meditating on them, contemplating—even singing them while trudging along the dusty roads of his times. When free he would hide in the most isolated parts of the monastery garden with his Bible and there remain in prayer reflecting on those sacred pages. At any time in his spiritual life he could linger with an image or painting of a scene from Christ's life and be lifted aloft. He taught that a holy image pictured in the mind or painted on a canvas or the sacred symbolic actions of the liturgy deserve to be prized because they can set the heart in motion toward the living image or mystery they represent.

As the heart begins to love the Lord, it delights in the least detail of his presence, his words, the scenes, the inexhaustible multiplicity of ways in which he reveals himself, especially in the Holy Scriptures. In these latter the Holy Spirit carries on a never-ending dialogue with us. As the heart is purified through these encounters, the words of Scripture begin to taste like honey and feel like fire.

This is the language and these the words God speaks in souls that are purged, cleansed, and all enkindled; as David exclaimed: *Your word is exceedingly enkindled* [Ps. 119:139]; and the prophet: *Are not my words, perchance, like a fire?* [Jer. 23:29]. As God himself says through St. John, these words are spirit and life [John 6:63]. These words are perceived by souls who have ears to hear them, those souls, as I say, that are cleansed and enamored. Those who do not have a sound palate, but seek other tastes, cannot taste the spirit and life of God's words; his words, rather, are distasteful to them.

Hence the loftier were the words of the Son of God, the more tasteless they were to the impure, as happened when he preached the sovereign and loving doctrine of the Holy Eucharist; for many turned away [John 6:60-61, 66].

Those who do not relish this language God speaks within them must not think on this account that others do not taste it. St. Peter tasted it in his soul when he said to Christ: *Lord, where shall we go; you have the words of eternal life* [John 6:68]. And the Samaritan woman forgot the water and the water pot for the sweetness of God's words [John 4:28]. (F 1.5–6)

# Chapter 5

# At the Threshold of Contemplation

As friendship with Christ grows, communion between the friends begins to predominate. The meditator begins to cherish being with Christ more than thinking about him, resting in his presence and receiving what he communicates, the pith or substance of meditation. But meditators may begin to feel they are idle, like lazy cats—doing nothing if not actively engaged in reading or working with their minds.

Many spiritual persons, after having exercised themselves in approaching God through images, forms, and meditations suitable for beginners, err greatly if they do not determine, dare, or know how to detach themselves from these palpable methods to which they are accustomed. (A 2.12.6)

## Contemplative Prayer and Contemplation

Nowadays the term "meditation" tends to be taken much more broadly than John of the Cross took it in his day. Exercises in which one repeats and dwells on a prayer word (or mantra), or focuses on breathing, or just passively watches the rise and fall of thoughts in the mind are what people may well think of when hearing the word meditation. Frequently the words "meditate" and "contemplate" are used interchangeably. But it wouldn't be wrong to hold that meditation usually suggests reflection on something and contemplation suggests looking at it attentively. As a result, some of the modern forms of meditation, if they are not merely secular exercises but carried out with Christian faith and purpose, could be classified as contemplative prayer.

John of the Cross, however, restricted the term "contemplation" to passive or "infused" prayer. But the *Catechism of the Catholic Church* speaks of contemplative prayer in the sense that St. Teresa of Avila gives to mental prayer: "an intimate sharing between friends; it means taking time to be alone with him who we know loves us" (2709). Contemplative prayer of this sort would be less likely to interfere with infused contemplation than would discursive meditation. Furthermore, for John of the Cross, discursive meditation unfolds into this close intimacy or communion between Christ and the soul.

In John's day, the Dominican Luis de Granada divided the steps of prayer in this manner: preparation, reading, meditation, thanksgiving, offering, and petition. The Carmelite followers of John, because of the wide use of these steps and the emphasis given by him to passivity, simplicity, and love, added contemplation as another step subsequent to meditation. In his capacity as councillor to the vicar general, John approved the first instruction for novices published in 1591, which includes contemplation as one of the steps of mental prayer. They also clarified that actual meditation need not always precede contemplation, since one who has habitual loving knowledge of the Beloved through truths arrived at in meditation enters easily into contemplation. Later Carmelites divided contemplation into acquired (a term never used by John) and infused, the former referring to the contemplation arrived at through meditation.

During the first half of the twentieth century a sometimes fiery argument emerged over the term "acquired contemplation." It had its roots in another dispute occasioned by a treatise on mystical theology by the Jesuit A. Poulain, entitled *The Graces of Interior Prayer*. Poulain asserted that an essential distinction must be made between the ascetical and mystical life, that the two do not constitute parts of one and the same way leading to perfection. Those who opposed him held that anyone journeying on the path to perfection would have to pass through both the ascetical and mystical life as two steps along one path. Many Carmelites sided with

Poulain, maintaining that acquired contemplation is the term of the prayer of those following the ascetical path and that perfection or union with God is reached by the people of this path when they live with their wills in complete conformity to God's will. Those journeying on the mystical path, in this view, experience the gift of infused contemplation in preparation for the mystical union of the spiritual marriage.

John does seem to allow for a stage between discursive meditation and passive prayer, for a prayer that is less active but not perceptively passive, although not as the term of an ascetical journey toward some kind of ascetical perfection.

Once the faculties reach the end of their journey they cease to work, just as we cease to walk when we reach the end of our journey. If everything consisted in going, one would never arrive; and if everywhere we found means, when and where could we enjoy the end and goal? ... If at times the soul puts the faculties to work, it should not use excessive efforts or studied reasonings, but it should proceed with gentleness of love, moved more by God than by its own abilities. (A 2.12.6.8)

We are at the threshold of contemplation, which for John is always infused, although the term "infused contemplation" could be misleading since all of God's self-communication is a gift and in a sense infused by him. How do we know, then, when contemplation is being given? We don't always know so easily, but perhaps knowing this is not as important as we might think. What is important is to know when to call a halt to the practice of a discursive form of meditation in prayer. In his prologue to the *Ascent* John describes the sorry situation that prodded him to write the book.

Sometimes they [those who practice discursive meditation] misunderstand themselves and are without suitable and alert directors who will show them the way to the summit. God gives many souls the talent and grace for advancing, and should they desire to make the effort they would arrive at this high state. And so it is sad to see them continue in their lowly method of communion with God because they do not want or know how to advance, or because they receive no direction on breaking away from the methods of beginners. (A prol. 3)

## Signs of Contemplation

To instruct his readers about when to renounce thinking and imaging in prayer, John elaborated three basic signs for indicating the advisability of setting aside the exercise of discursive meditation.

Hence we will delineate some signs and indications by which one can judge whether or not it is the opportune time for the spiritual person to discontinue meditation.

The first is the realization that one cannot make discursive meditation or receive satisfaction from it as before. Dryness is now the outcome of fixing the senses on subjects that formerly provided satisfaction. However, as long as one can make discursive meditation and draw out satisfaction, one must not abandon this method. Meditation must be discontinued only when the soul is placed in that peace and quietude to be spoken of in the third sign.

The second sign is an awareness of a disinclination to fix the imagination or sense faculties on other particular objects, exterior or interior. I am not affirming that the imagination will cease to come and go—even in deep recollection it usually wanders freely—but that the person does not want to fix it purposely on extraneous things.

The third and surest sign is that a person likes to remain alone in loving awareness of God, without particular considerations, in interior peace and quiet and repose, and without the acts and exercises (at least discursive, those in which one progresses from point to point) of the intellect, memory and will. Such a one prefers to remain only in the general, loving awareness and knowledge we mentioned, without any particular knowledge or understanding. (A 2.13.1–4)

Negatively speaking, no more satisfaction comes from the old procedure. But no desire to surrender the time of prayer for other pursuits is present either. The inclination is to remain in the simple communion with God to which the discursive meditation should lead.

Two other points from John's teaching here need highlighting: One is that the mind may wander to and fro during contemplative prayer; this unwilled nuisance is not an impediment to God's communication. The other is that some nondiscursive practices of meditation, like the slow repetition of a prayer, said without compulsion, need not be renounced because in themselves they do not hinder the receptivity required for contemplation the way discursive activity does.

### The Spiritual Vices of Beginners

In John's analysis, the gratification felt by beginners adds a heavy weight in the scale toward their conversion, and consolation may take hold of them not only in prayer but in their newly discovered good works as well. But consolation has the potential also to sow the seed for a different variety of faults and sins as the former one fades. Attachment to the pleasures of religion has the potential to block the path to union with God as much as attachment to money, beauty, and sensual pleasures does.

The list of capital sins presented John with a tool for examining the faults deriving from spiritual consolations. The list of seven goes back to the experience of the Egyptian desert monks: pride, envy, anger, sloth, avarice, gluttony, and lust. In the "Parson's Tale" of Chaucer's *Canterbury Tales*, the sermon relates the capital sins to our day-to-day life. They "are all leashed together," says the Parson; these sins are "the trunk of the tree from which others branch." John of the Cross uncovers them even in such apparently edifying places as our prayer, spiritual practices, and good works. Are there any religious persons, even though they may not think they are beginners, who would not meet themselves somewhere in his straightforward depictions?

For a clearer understanding of this and of how truly imperfect beginners are, insofar as they practice virtue readily because of the satisfaction attached to it, we will describe, using the seven capital vices as our basis, some of the numerous imperfections beginners commit. Thus we will clearly see how very similar their deeds are to those of children.

These beginners feel so fervent and diligent in their spiritual exercises and undertakings that a certain kind of secret pride is generated in them which begets a complacency with themselves and their accomplishments, despite the fact that holy works do of their very nature cause humility. Then they develop a desire somewhat vain—at times very vain—to speak of spiritual things in others' presence, and sometimes even to instruct rather than be instructed; in their hearts they condemn others who do not seem to have the kind of devotion they would like them to have, and sometimes they give expression to this criticism like the pharisee who despised the publican while he boasted and praised God for the good deeds he himself accomplished [Luke 18:11–12].

The devil, desiring the growth of pride and presumption in these beginners, often increases their fervor and readiness to perform such works, and other ones, too. For he is quite aware of the fact that all these works and virtues are not only worthless for them, but even become vices. Some of these persons become so evil-minded that they do not want anyone except themselves to appear holy; and so by both word and deed, they condemn and detract others whenever the occasion arises, seeing the little splinter in their brother's eye, and failing to consider the wooden beam in their own eye [Matt. 7:3]; they strain at the other's gnat and swallow their own camel [Matt. 23:24]. (N 1.1.3–2.2)

Many beginners also at times possess great spiritual avarice. They will hardly ever seem content with the spirit God gives them. They become unhappy and peevish because they don't find the consolation they want in spiritual things. Many never have enough of hearing counsels, or of learning spiritual maxims, or of keeping them and reading books about them. They spend more time in these than in striving after mortification and the perfection of the interior poverty to which they are obliged.

Furthermore, they weigh themselves down with overdecorated images and rosaries. They now put these down, now take up others; at one moment they are exchanging, and at the next re-exchanging. Now they want this kind, now they want another. And they prefer one cross to another because of its elaborateness. Others you see decked out in *Agnus Dei*s and relics and lists of saints' names, like children in trinkets. (N 1.3.1)

Some people are so delicate that when gratification is received spiritually, or in prayer, they immediately experience a lust that so inebriates them and caresses their senses that they become as it were engulfed in the delight and satisfaction of that vice; and this experience will continue passively with the other. Sometimes these individuals become aware that certain impure and rebellious acts have taken place. The reason for such occurrences is that since these natures are, as I say, delicate and tender, their humors and blood are stirred up by any change. These persons will also experience such feelings when they are inflamed with anger or agitated by some other disturbance or affliction.

Some spiritually acquire a liking for other individuals that often arises from lust rather than from the spirit. This lustful origin will be recognized if, on recalling that affection, there is remorse of conscience, not an increase in the remembrance and love of God. (N 1.4.5.7)

Because of the strong desire of many beginners for spiritual gratification, they usually have many imperfections of anger. When the delight and satisfaction procured in their spiritual exercises passes, these beginners are naturally left without any spiritual savor. And because of this distastefulness, they become peevish in the works they do and easily angered by the least thing, and occasionally they are so unbearable that nobody can put up with them. This frequently occurs after they have experienced in prayer some recollection pleasant to the senses. After the delight and satisfaction is gone, the sensory part of the soul is naturally left vapid and zestless, just as a child is when withdrawn from the sweet breast. These souls are not at fault if they do not allow this dejection to influence

them, for it is an imperfection that must be purged through the
dryness and distress of the dark night.

Among these spiritual persons there are also those who fall
into another kind of spiritual anger. Through a certain indiscreet
zeal they become angry over the sins of others, reprove these
others, and sometimes even feel the impulse to do so angrily,
which in fact they occasionally do, setting themselves up as
lords of virtue. All such conduct is contrary to spiritual meekness.

Others, in becoming aware of their own imperfections, grow
angry with themselves in an unhumble impatience. So impa-
tient are they about these imperfections that they would want
to become saints in a day. Many of these beginners will make
numerous plans and great resolutions, but since they are not
humble and have no distrust of themselves, the more resolves
they make the more they break, and the greater becomes their
anger. (N 1.5.1–3)

A great deal can be said on spiritual gluttony, the fourth
vice. There are hardly any persons among these beginners, no
matter how excellent their conduct, who do not fall into some
of the many imperfections of this vice. These imperfections
arise because of the delight beginners find in their spiritual
exercises.

Many, lured by the delight and satisfaction procured in their
religious practices, strive more for spiritual savor than for spiritual purity and discretion; yet it is this purity and discretion
that God looks for and finds acceptable throughout a soul's
entire spiritual journey. Besides the imperfection of seeking after
these delights, the sweetness these persons experience makes
them go to extremes and pass beyond the mean in which
virtue resides and is acquired. Some, attracted by the delight
they feel in their spiritual exercises, kill themselves with
penances, and others weaken themselves by fasts and, without
the counsel or command of another, overtax their weakness;
indeed they try to hide these penances from the one to whom
they owe obedience in such matters. Some will even dare perform these penances contrary to obedience.

Such individuals are unreasonable and most imperfect. They subordinate submissiveness and obedience (which is a penance of reason and discretion, and consequently a sacrifice more pleasing and acceptable to God) to corporeal penance. But corporeal penance without obedience is no more than a penance of beasts. And like beasts, they are motivated in these penances by an appetite for the pleasure they find in them. Since all extremes are vicious and since by such behavior these persons are doing their own will, they grow in vice rather than in virtue. For through this conduct they at least become spiritually gluttonous and proud, since they do not tread the path of obedience. (N 2.6.1–2)

As for the other two vices, spiritual envy and sloth, these beginners also have many imperfections. In regard to envy, many of them feel sad about the spiritual good of others and experience sensible grief in noting that their neighbor is ahead of them on the road to perfection, and they will not want to hear others praised. Learning of the virtues of others makes them sad. They cannot bear to hear others being praised without contradicting and undoing these compliments as much as possible. Their annoyance grows because they themselves do not receive these plaudits and because they long for preference in everything. All of this is contrary to charity, which, as St. Paul says, *rejoices in the truth* [1 Cor. 13:6]. (N 1.7.1)

Also, regarding spiritual sloth, these beginners usually become weary in exercises that are more spiritual and flee from them since these exercises are contrary to sensory satisfaction. Since they are so used to finding delight in spiritual practices, they become bored when they do not find it. If they do not receive in prayer the satisfaction they crave—for after all it is fit that God withdraw this so as to try them—they do not want to return to it, or at times they either give up prayer or go to it begrudgingly. Because of their sloth, they subordinate the way of perfection (which requires denying one's own will and satisfaction for God) to the pleasure and delight of their own will. As a result they strive to satisfy their own will rather than God's. (N 1.7.1)

Many of these beginners want God to desire what they want, and they become sad if they have to desire God's will. They feel an aversion toward adapting their will to God's. Hence they frequently believe that what is not their will, or that which brings them no satisfaction, is not God's will, and, on the other hand, that if they are satisfied, God is too. They measure God by themselves and not themselves by God, which is in opposition to his teaching in the Gospel, that those who lose their life for his sake will gain it and that those who desire to gain it will lose it [Matt. 16:25]. (N 1.7.2)

Although John is painstaking in his treatment of these imperfections, he is convinced that no one could be rid of them solely through personal effort.

Yet until a soul is placed by God in the passive purgation of that dark night, which we will soon explain, it cannot purify itself completely of these imperfections or from the others. But people should insofar as possible strive to do their part in purifying and perfecting themselves and thereby merit God's divine cure. In this cure God will heal them of what through their own efforts they were unable to remedy. No matter how much individuals do through their own efforts, they cannot actively purify themselves enough to be disposed in the least degree for the divine union of the perfection of love. God must take over and purge them in that fire that is dark for them, as we will explain. (N 1.3.3)

### Gradual Transitions

It should be no surprise that people will experience gratification through the spiritual practices that are most suited to them, whether this be through discursive meditation or other simpler forms of contemplative prayer. Discussing the signs in the *Ascent of Mount Carmel* that indicate the appropriate time for setting aside reading and discursive meditation, or other busy activity in prayer, John leaves the impression that one begins to experience at once an infused contemplation in "interior peace and quiet and repose." Ordinarily, however, contemplation as a habitual mode of prayer enters the scene only gradually.

In the measure that souls approach spirit in their dealings with God, they divest and empty themselves of the ways of the senses, of discursive and imaginative meditation. When they have completely attained spiritual communion with God, they will be void of all sensory apprehensions concerning God. The more an object approaches one extreme, the further it retreats from the other; on complete attainment of the one extreme, it will be wholly separated from the other. There is a frequently quoted spiritual axiom that runs: Once the taste and savor of the spirit is experienced, everything carnal is insipid. The ways of the flesh (which refer to the use of the senses in spiritual things) afford neither profit nor delight. This is obvious. If something is spiritual, it is incomprehensible to the senses; but if the senses can grasp it, it is no longer purely spiritual. The more knowledge the senses and natural apprehensions have about it, the less spiritual and supernatural it will be. (A 2.17.4–5)

In the search through reading, the discovery through discursive meditation, the knocking in prayer (mental prayer, also called now contemplative prayer), and the opening of the door in "infused" contemplation, the transition to the latter does not come easily. Accustomed as we are to material objects, it is difficult to turn from such props and enter the delicate world of spiritual reality. What John means by infused contemplation is that the loving knowledge is communicated directly to the spirit, without particular images and ideas as means. Without these palpable means, contemplation comes divested of the particular and is therefore a general, or obscure, loving knowledge. It is God's life, his self-communication; in us it is the life of the theological virtues of which we will speak in the next chapter.

In the Hebrew mind "the blood is the life" (Deut. 12:23). To be sprinkled with blood means to be in contact with life, with Yahweh's life, to be purified and reconsecrated to God. In this sense Christ "entered once for all into the Holy Place, taking not the blood of goats or calves but his own blood . . . how much more shall the blood of Christ . . . purify your consciences from dead works to serve the living God" (Heb. 9:12–14). It is the life of Christ that cleanses and purifies us at the same time that it works to bring about complete union. This is why contemplation is not only illuminative and unitive but also purgative.

Purgative contemplation, initially purging the senses and accommodating them to spirit, is what John calls the passive night. In practical terms what happens is that the life of Christ to which one had so happily converted becomes distasteful both in prayer and in good works.

For it is through the delight and satisfaction they [beginners] experience in prayer that they have become detached from worldly things and have gained some spiritual strength in God. This strength has helped them somewhat to restrain their appetites for creatures, and through it they will be able to suffer a little oppression and dryness without turning back. Consequently, it is at the time they are going about their spiritual exercises with delight and satisfaction, when in their opinion the sun of divine favor is shining most brightly on them, that God darkens all this light. . . . God now leaves them in such darkness that they do not know which way to turn in their discursive imaginings. They cannot advance a step in meditation, as they used to, now that the interior sense faculties are engulfed in this night. He leaves them in such dryness that they not only fail to receive satisfaction and pleasure from their spiritual exercises and works, as they formerly did, but also find these exercises distasteful and bitter. As I said, when God sees that they have grown a little, he weans them from the sweet breast so that they might be strengthened, lays aside their swaddling bands, and puts them down from his arms that they may grow accustomed to walking by themselves. This change is a surprise to them because everything seems to be functioning in reverse. . . . Not much time ordinarily passes after the initial stages of their spiritual life before beginners start to enter this night of sense. And the majority of them do enter it because it is common to see them suffer these aridities. (N 1.8.3, 5)

# Chapter 6

# As a Mother Weans Her Child

As a mother weans her child, God, according to John of the Cross, weans souls from the sweet breast of consolation, lays aside their swaddling bands, and puts them down from her arms that they may learn to walk sturdily by themselves. God it is, then, who initiates the change from sense to spirit, from active to passive prayer.

### Body and Soul

When speaking of sense and spirit, or of nights or purgations of the senses and spirit, John assumes some standard truths about the soul. In addition to the fact that the soul does not, as was mentioned, have being independent of the body, but is a single entity of a composite nature, a unity with the body, it may be added that the soul is the life-giving principle of the body, the principle of all vital activities. Since the soul performs different kinds of activities, the statement is often made that it has different parts, a part for each kind of activity. But since a soul is not a material body, these parts cannot be quantitative parts, as when we divide a book into two parts. When John speaks of parts of the soul, he is referring to its kinds of activity.

These parts are nothing else than the powers, or faculties, the opportunities the soul has for performing different sorts of life activity. When we say that the soul is divisible into parts, the meaning is simply that these parts are distinguishable from each other by definition, since each may be defined in terms of its

116

object. The object of seeing is color, or hearing, sound, and so on. Now the power of seeing is an act of the bodily eye and the power of hearing is an act of the bodily ear. But none of the bodily organs can think. The human soul is distinguished from the souls of other living things by virtue of its having this thinking part or power. This power was called a rational soul by Aristotle.

John often uses the words "spirit" and "soul" interchangeably. What is spirit, then? He would have us think of it as the non-material aspect of ourselves, the more-than-bodily me that I refer to when I speak of myself as having a body rather than being a body. Matter and spirit are clearly distinct kinds of reality. Matter can be measured and weighed; spirit cannot. You can cut your fingernails but you cannot cut off any part of your spirit. If you fly to Milwaukee, your spirit goes with you, because the human spirit is an embodied spirit. But the body is not a prison for the soul, nor is the soul in the body as the body may be in a house materially, nor is the soul less real than matter. It is difficult for us to think about the spirit, and since John of the Cross writes so much about the spirit, he is often puzzling to read.

Odd as it may seem, our bodies are in our souls. Spirits cannot be contained in bodies because they cannot be contained in a material way, but bodies can be contained in spirits in a spiritual way; they are a part of the spirit's identity, meaning, and life. What is more, the spirit, having its source in God, is in God spiritually.

A lover can never be satisfied with a superficial apprehension of the beloved but wants to gain an intimate knowledge of everything pertaining to the beloved, to penetrate into the beloved's very soul. So it is written of the Holy Spirit, who is God's Love, that the Spirit searches all, yes even the deep things of God (1 Cor. 2:10).

Bodily sight is the beginning of sensitive love; similarly the contemplation of spiritual beauty or goodness is the beginning of spiritual love. The lover of Christ, on this account, could never be satisfied with a knowledge of him bound to the senses, that is, to the particular; or be nonchalant about a sensitive love. The Beloved then begins to draw the loving disciple to a level of

*Avidity*

deeper intimacy, to the elusive level of spirit, a transition that provokes a crisis. The constricted way to the light and love of the spirit lies through the desert. The ordinary person is too taken up with the coarse noise of the material world to move easily into the delicate stillness of spiritual experience.

### Initial Contemplation

John of the Cross calls God's new way of self-communication initial contemplation; it is hardly perceptible—perhaps even imperceptible—in the beginning, for the movement from meditation beyond the visible world to contemplation need not be dramatic.

Actually, at the beginning of this state the loving knowledge is almost unnoticeable. There are two reasons for this: first, the loving knowledge initially is likely to be extremely subtle and delicate, and almost imperceptible; second, a person who is habituated to the exercise of meditation, which is wholly sensible, hardly perceives or feels this new insensible, purely spiritual experience. This is especially so when through failure to understand it one does not permit oneself to rest in it but strives after the other more sensory experience. Although the interior peace is more abundant, the individual allows no room for its experience and enjoyment. But the more habituated persons become to this calm, the more their experience of this general, loving knowledge of God will increase. (A 2.13.7)

John did not describe this stage in the *Ascent;* it was his intention there to explain the first stage of infused contemplation when expounding the passive purifications. What he teaches about infused contemplation in the *Ascent* is generally more suited to experiences that follow the passive night of the senses. In the passive night of the senses "the senses are purged and accommodated to the spirit" through the drudgery of aridity in prayer. Dryness, or aridity, denotes a lack of water. Metaphorically, then, spiritual dryness is a condition in which the former sensory consolation and joy have fallen away.

The reason for this dryness is that God transfers his goods and strength from sense to spirit. Since the sensory part of the soul is incapable of the goods of spirit, it remains deprived, dry, and empty. Thus, while the spirit is tasting, the flesh tastes nothing at all and becomes weak in its work. But through this nourishment the spirit grows stronger and more alert, and becomes more solicitous than before about not failing God.

If in the beginning the soul does not experience this spiritual savor and delight, but dryness and distaste, the reason is the novelty involved in this exchange. Since its palate is accustomed to these other sensory tastes, the soul still sets its eyes on them. And since, also, its spiritual palate is neither purged nor accommodated for so subtle a taste, it is unable to experience the spiritual savor and good until gradually prepared by means of this dark and obscure night. The soul instead experiences dryness and distaste because of a lack of the gratification it formerly enjoyed so readily.

Those whom God begins to lead into these desert solitudes are like the children of Israel. When God began giving them the heavenly food, which contained in itself all savors and changed to whatever taste each one hungered after [Wis. 16:20–21], as is there mentioned, they nonetheless felt a craving for the tastes of the fleshmeats and onions they had eaten in Egypt, for their palate was accustomed and attracted to them more than to the delicate sweetness of the angelic manna. And in the midst of that heavenly food, they wept and sighed for fleshmeat [Num. 11:4–6]. The baseness of our appetite is such that it makes us long for our own miserable goods and feel aversion for the incommunicable heavenly good.

Yet, as I say, when these aridities are the outcome of the purgative way of the sensory appetite, the spirit feels the strength and energy to work, which is obtained from the substance of that interior food, even though in the beginning, for the reason just mentioned, it may not experience the savor. This food is the beginning of a contemplation that is dark and dry to the senses. Ordinarily this contemplation, which is secret and hidden from the very one who receives it, imparts to the soul,

together with the dryness and emptiness it produces in the
senses, an inclination to remain alone and in quietude. And the
soul will be unable to dwell on any particular thought, nor will
it have the desire to do so.... This food is the beginning of a
contemplation that is dark and dry to the senses.... (N 1.9.4–5)

## Wrestling with Aridity

Understandably, if I desire to persevere in prayer despite the
absence of satisfaction, the question keeps posing itself whether
I myself am not to blame for being lost in the waste hills without
the consolations of love. But a shuddering at the thought of having lost the Beloved and a solicitude about what to do are themselves the signs of God's communication, the manner in which
love here reveals its face. John distinguishes between a dryness
resulting from God's purgative contemplation and a pointless
dryness caused by mediocrity:

The second sign for the discernment of this purgation is that
the memory ordinarily turns to God solicitously and with painful
care, and the soul thinks it is not serving God but turning back,
because it is aware of this distaste for the things of God.
Hence it is obvious that this aversion and dryness is not the
fruit of laxity and tepidity, for lukewarm people do not care
much for the things of God nor are they inwardly solicitous
about them.
    There is, consequently, a notable difference between dryness
and lukewarmness. The lukewarm are very lax and remiss in
their will and spirit, and have no solicitude about serving God.
Those suffering from the purgative dryness are ordinarily solicitous, concerned, and pained about not serving God. (N 1.9.3)

Among the most common experiences in the spiritual life,
aridity can, like clouds, blow in at any time. It need not be
restricted by us to those particular periods of transition in the
spiritual life that John describes when treating of the passive
night of the senses or the passive night of the spirit. He always

insists that we allow for much variety in anyone's experience. Aridity is an experience that comes not just in prayer; it may pervade the whole of one's life and accompany the works of service performed for God and other human beings. The only problem with aridity lies with those who experience it, their inclination to think that if they receive no consolation or satisfaction, nothing beneficial is happening.

Aridity in prayer will also make one more aware of distractions, adding to the feeling that the prayer serves no purpose, is a waste of time. Aridity gives the impression that God is distant, unimpressed by and unconcerned with spiritual seekers as they think of their lost, imagined renown. Aridity will make those who suffer from it conjecture that they have come up against a dead end, that they are lukewarm in their spiritual life, that they have no zeal. They hear voices urging "let us return to self-seeking."

John of the Cross prized aridity and for himself preferred it. He made a determined effort to convince his readers of its worth. It is good for the soul in all stages of the spiritual life. After all, Christ on the cross was steeped in aridity at an hour in which his prayer was more powerful than in those lone nights in the stillness of the mountains.

At the moment of his death he was certainly annihilated in his soul, without any consolation or relief, since the Father had left him that way in innermost aridity in the lower part. He was thereby compelled to cry out: "My God, My God, why have you forsaken me"? [Matt. 27:46]. This was the most extreme abandonment, sensitively, that he had suffered in his life. And by it he accomplished the most marvelous work of his whole life, surpassing all the works and deeds and miracles that he had ever performed on earth or in heaven. That is, he brought about the reconciliation and union of the human race with God through grace. (A 2.7.11)

It is difficult to measure the pulse of one's prayer, for it is difficult to judge the quality of one's love; love is unidentifiable with feelings of love. Love in aridity can be a more intense love than love in ecstasy.

It must be confessed, and John admits, that aridity may have its source in sin, imperfection, and lukewarmness. But such a condition, for one thing, would only disclose a stronger need for prayer and good works, for perseverance in the best way possible, perhaps a need to make changes in the dull routine of one's daily habits.

If aridity is occasioned by melancholia (depression) or other sickness, these can serve to purify the soul also; yet one must seek help or treatment for the illness insofar as possible. Capable of incapacitating us totally, an illness can contribute to the experience of aridity, but would do no spiritual harm to the one who accepts it with loving patience and resignation to God's will. Aridity can always serve for our purification and sanctification provided our attitude toward it is correct. In itself it presents no cause for worry, even if its source may lie somewhere else than in purgative contemplation.

It is noteworthy that, however elevated God's communications and the experiences of his presence are, and however sublime a person's knowledge of him may be, these are not God essentially, nor are they comparable to him because, indeed, he is still hidden to the soul. Hence, regardless of all these lofty experiences, a person should think of him as hidden and seek him as one who is hidden, saying: "Where have You hidden?"

Neither the sublime communication nor the sensible awareness of [God's] nearness are a sure testimony of his gracious presence, nor are dryness and the lack of these a reflection of his absence. As a result, the prophet Job exclaims: "If he comes to me I shall not see him, and if he goes away I shall not understand" [Job 9:11].

It must be understood that if a person experiences some elevated spiritual communication or feeling or knowledge, it should not be thought that the experiences are similar to the clear and essential vision or possession of God, or that the communication, no matter how remarkable it is, signifies a more notable possession of God or union with him. It should be known too that if all these sensible and spiritual communications are wanting and individuals live in dryness, darkness, and dereliction, they must not thereby think that God is any more absent than in the former case. People, actually, cannot have certain knowledge from the one state that they are in God's grace or from the other that they are not. As the Wise Man says, "We do not know if we are worthy of love or abhorrence before God" [Eccl. 9:1]. (C 1.3–4)

When solicitude about serving God and the fear of having gone astray are present, John insists that there is no need to try to backtrack to former methods if there is no inclination to do so. An essential requirement for John when prayer and other good works are prey to aridity is patient perseverance. To this may be added a counsel of equal importance: "Trust in God who does not fail those who seek him with a simple and righteous heart" (N 1.10.3). In what way will God not fail? He will not fail to give a person everything needed to reach the journey's end, which is transformation in Christ in clear and pure light.

Contemplation requires a receptive mode liberated from anxieties about accomplishment, a freedom of spirit able to cut ties with the urge to be engaged in reading and studious reflections, with ideas and images. One may think that the time of aridity and distraction could be better spent preparing for Bible-study class. On the contrary, during the time reserved for this arid prayer

they must be content simply with a loving and peaceful attentiveness to God, and live without the concern, without the effort, and without the desire to taste or feel him. All these desires disquiet the soul and distract it from the peaceful, quiet, and sweet idleness of the contemplation that is being communicated to it. (N 1.10.4)

Efforts to drive out dryness and produce stillness and quiet easily lead to more dryness. Prayer is a time to be at peace in God's presence, in a desire to be attentive to the divine presence in a general, receptive, and loving way.

And even though more scruples come to the fore concerning the loss of time and the advantages of doing something else, since it cannot do anything or think of anything in prayer, the soul should endure them peacefully, as though going to prayer means remaining in ease and freedom of spirit. If individuals were to desire to do something themselves with their interior faculties, they would hinder and lose the goods which God engraves on their souls through that peace and idleness. If a model for the painting or retouching of a portrait should move because of a desire to do something, the artist would be unable to finish, and the work would be spoiled. Similarly, any operation, affection, or advertence a soul might desire when it wants to abide in interior peace and idleness would cause distraction and disquietude, and make it feel sensory dryness and emptiness. The more a person seeks some support in knowledge and affection the more the soul will feel the lack of these, for this support cannot be supplied through these sensory means. (N 1.10.5)

Groping perceptions of powerlessness and weakness can induce a crisis, but weakness stirs up the power of God, becomes the occasion for calling on the Spirit whom the Father gives to all those who ask. The secret for a soul is to allow itself to be led by the Spirit. The Spirit will come not only to help our weakness but also to pray within us and with us, reaching beyond our limited attempts, interceding for us with ineffable sighs. Yet one's desires may still be too superficial and immature. The waiting, the purification, the night are necessary for convincing individuals of the desires of the Spirit until, like dry earth soaking up the rain, they allow themselves to be penetrated totally and their sighs to be identical with the Spirit's.

The fire of love is not commonly felt at the outset, either because it does not have a chance to take hold, owing to the impurity of the sensory part, or because the soul for want of understanding has not made within itself a peaceful place for it; although at times with or without these conditions a person will begin to feel a certain longing for God. (N 1.11.1)

This is the secret of prayer: to allow oneself to be led by the Spirit. Prayer must not be cast as a struggle to think only of God or to create a void and discard distractions. In the poverty of dryness and distraction one must remain before the divine Friend with all one's life exposed, all the whirling thoughts and images that are there. Prayer must be truthful corresponding to the reality one carries within oneself, however miserable. If we satisfy ourselves with nice thoughts about God and believe that we are achieving something, we may be deceiving ourselves. Our concerns and concrete life are not what sets us apart from God, but our not knowing how to place our lives in God's hands and behold them with God's eyes. This is not just another method of concentration, but something necessary for prayer to be Christian. Anyone who reaches total interior silence knows that it is not the consequence of a prolonged struggle to create a vacuum of all things, but the consequence of an effort to live only for God and to place all one's life in God's hands.

## The Benefits of Aridity

Distraction, dryness, the experience of weakness can bring forth an unexpected yield. Through earthly and heavenly satisfactions a person can stumble into any number of faults from the capital sins; this has been made clear. In depriving the soil of water, the dryness reduces weeds and mold, allows for cultivation, and occasions the fruitfulness of many blessings. The first and chief benefit is knowledge of self, the truth about oneself in the light of God.

It considers itself to be nothing and finds no satisfaction in self because it is aware that of itself it neither does nor can do anything. God esteems this lack of self-satisfaction and the dejection persons have about not serving him more than all their former deeds and gratifications, however notable they may have been, since they were the occasion of many imperfections and a great deal of ignorance. (N 1.12.2)

A deeper reverence and humility before God ensue, as in the case of Moses, who in leaving aside his sandals became fully aware of his misery in the sight of God. And not until Job was seated on the dunghill did God descend to speak to him and reveal the mysteries of the divine wisdom.

When the sensory appetites, gratifications, and supports are quenched, the intellect is left clean and free to understand the truth, for even though these appetites and pleasures concern spiritual things they blind and impede the spirit. Similarly the anguish and dryness of the senses illumine and quicken the intellect, as Isaiah affirms: "vexation makes one understand" [Isa. 28:19]. But God also, by means of this dark and dry night of contemplation, supernaturally instructs in his divine wisdom the soul that is empty and unhindered (which is the requirement for his divine inpouring), which he did not do through the former satisfactions and pleasures. (N 1.12.4)

3)   With the resulting humility, the aimless tendency to compare oneself to others as more advanced loses its foothold. Surprisingly, John had little to say about the most prevalent theme of all preaching: love of neighbor. This could be attributed to his concern to deal mainly with matters he thought were not covered sufficiently in other books. But perhaps also his neglect of this topic owed something to his clear observation of how easy it is for people to think they are superior to their neighbor because of their love of neighbor. John was convinced that an authentic love of neighbor would be active in the measure that humility and love of God were present, for love of neighbor is the close companion of humility.

From this humility stems love of neighbor, for they will esteem them and not judge them as they did before when they were aware that they enjoyed an intense fervor while others did not.

These persons will know only their own misery and keep it so much in sight that they will have no opportunity to watch anyone else's conduct. David while in this night gives an admirable manifestation of such a state of soul: "I became dumb, and was humbled, and I kept silent in good things, and my sorrow was renewed" [Ps. 39:2]. He says this because it seemed to him that his blessings had so come to an end that not only was he unable to find words for them, but he also became silent concerning his neighbor, in the sorrow he experienced from the knowledge of his own misery.

These individuals also become submissive and obedient in their spiritual journey. Since they are so aware of their own wretchedness, they not only listen to the teaching of others but even desire to be directed and told what to do by anyone at all. (N 1.12.7–8)

 Other benefits are that such persons become more temperate in their spiritual exercises, more peaceful, patient, persevering, and strong; their passions lessen in intensity. They respond with untroubled meekness toward their neighbor and are happy to accept the success of others.

 These aridities, then, make people walk with purity in the love of God. No longer are they moved to act by the delight and satisfaction they find in a work, as they perhaps were when they derived this from their deeds, but by the desire of pleasing God. They are neither presumptuous nor self-satisfied, as was their custom in the time of their prosperity, but fearful and disquieted about themselves and lacking in any self-satisfaction. This is the holy fear which preserves and gives increase to the virtues. (N 1.13.12)

In a word, they increase in all the theological and moral virtues. It is by a path in which things seem to be falling apart,  certainly a path you never expect, that the Christian becomes configured to Christ. The moment has come now to see how John explains the theological principles of infused contemplation.

# Chapter 7

# The Path of the Spirit

For when once the will
is touched by God himself,
it cannot find contentment
except in the Divinity;
but since his Beauty is open
to faith alone, the will
*tastes him in I-don't-know-what*
*which is so gladly found.* (P 12.5)

The purification wrought by aridity prepares one to enter what John calls "the path of the spirit," or "the way of proficients," "the way of infused contemplation," or "the illuminative way." How does one walk along this way? By becoming blind, by walking in faith.

In this way, in obscurity, souls approach union swiftly by means of faith, which is also dark. And in this way faith gives them wondrous light. Obviously, if they should desire to see, they would be in darkness as regards God more quickly than anyone who looks to see the blinding brightness of the sun.

By blinding one's faculties along this road, one will see light, as the Savior proclaims in the Gospel: I have come into this world for judgment, that those who see not, may see, and that those who see may become blind [John 9:39]. In reference to the spiritual road, these words should be understood literally, that is: Those who both live in darkness and blind themselves of all their natural lights will have supernatural

128

vision, and those who want to lean on some light of their own will become blind and be held back on this road leading to union. (A 2.4.6–7)

It is time to delve further into the meaning of spirit, contemplation, and faith. In the previous chapter I presented some thoughts about the spirit and how it is the nonmaterial aspect of the human subject. Besides referring to the spirit in this sense, John also speaks of spirit as the loving knowledge of God given to the soul in contemplation.

In the measure that souls approach spirit in their dealings with God, they divest and empty themselves of the ways of the senses, of discursive and imaginative meditation.... There is a frequently quoted spiritual axiom that runs: *Gustato spiritu, disipit omnis caro* (Once the taste and savor of the spirit is experienced, everything carnal is insipid). (A 2.17.5)

For another example we can skip to stanza 3 in the *Living Flame of Love:*

These directors do not know what spirit is. They do a great injury to God and show disrespect toward him by intruding with a rough hand where he is working. It cost God a great deal to bring these souls to this stage, and he highly values his work of having introduced them into this solitude and emptiness regarding their faculties and activity so that he might speak to their hearts, which is what he always desires. Since he it is who now reigns in the soul with an abundance of peace and calm, he takes the initiative himself by making the natural acts of the faculties fail, by which the soul laboring the whole night accomplished nothing [Luke 5:5]; and he feeds the spirit without the activity of the senses because neither the sense nor its function is capable of spirit. (54)

One cannot always be certain whether the term "spirit" as used by John refers to God and therefore requires capitalization of the first letter. The decision must be made on the basis of the context. What interests us here is the question of the link between link between

the "spirit" taken as God's self-communication and the "spirit"
taken as the receiver of the contemplation.

## The Intellect

The external and internal senses are means by which we function
at the level of both the senses and the material creation. We can
easily conclude that, since we can see and hear and picture things
to ourselves, we have powers, or faculties, for doing such things.
But as human beings we also find ourselves doing what cannot
be performed through these sensory powers. Plato and Aristotle,
and their followers, make a distinction in kind between sensa-
tions or images and universal ideas or abstract concepts. Sense
and intellect are for them distinct faculties of knowing and have
distinct objects of knowledge.

John of the Cross followed the classic philosophy that came
down from Aristotle and Aquinas. The intellect is our power of
thinking and knowing. But there are many differences among
philosophers about the activities of thinking. Aristotle initiated a
distinction between the mind as an active and as a passive power.
This was more explicitly formulated by Aquinas in his theory of
the active intellect and the intellect as potential. The human intellect, Aquinas writes, "is in potentiality to things intelligible. . . .
At first we are only potentiality toward understanding, and afterward we are made to understand actually. And so it is evident
that with us to understand is in a way to be passive." But the
forms (concepts) of things, or what Aquinas calls their "intelligible species," are not actually intelligible as they exist in material
things. He therefore argues that in addition to the "power receptive of such species, which is called the 'possible intellect' by reason of its being potentiality to such species," there must be
another intellectual power, which he calls the active or "agent"
intellect. Nothing, he says, can be reduced from potentiality to
act except by something "in act" (already actual). "We must
therefore assign on the part of the intellect some power to make
things actually intelligible, by the abstraction of the species from

material conditions. Such is the necessity for positing an agent intellect."

The intellectual power that is receptive of the intelligible species may be in complete potentiality to them, as it is when it has not yet come to understand certain things. Or it may be in habitual possession of the intelligible species: it has previously acquired the understanding of certain things but is not now actually engaged in understanding them. In the third place, the potential intellect may also be actual or in act whenever it is actually exercising its habit of understanding or is for the first time actually understanding something.

Among all bodily forms, the human soul alone has the distinction of possessing an operation and a power in which corporeal matter has no share whatever. But Aquinas also maintains, as was mentioned in chapter 4, that the body is necessary for the action of the intellect, not as its organ of action, but on the part of the object: the phantasm or image produced by the sensory faculty.

This thinking about our human thinking, about what we know and how we know it, has stirred up a maze of debates, many of them coming after John of the Cross wrote. Furthermore the study of the subject has now become quite different, for the interest has shifted to the study of oneself inasmuch as one is conscious. It prescinds from the soul, its essence, its potencies, its habits, for none of these are given in consciousness. It discerns the different levels of consciousness: of the dreamer, of the waking, intelligently inquiring, rationally reflecting, or responsibly deliberating subject. But the fact that knowledge involves a relationship between a knower and a known seems to go undisputed. What can be said of John of the Cross is that for him reality was one thing and his thought about reality another. He held that through the use of our minds we can know reality; our thoughts can express what really is. Moreover, this presupposes that some thoughts are correct and others are not, that some agree with reality and others are mere delusion. Finally some correct thoughts are more complete than others that, though correct, are less complete.

## Mystical Knowledge

If it has been so troubling a problem for philosophers to come to agreement on how we have knowledge of the corporeal world around us, how can one hope to speak intelligibly of mystical knowledge? Mystical knowledge is a knowledge received without sense images (sensible forms or species) or particular ideas (intelligible forms or species) and without the process of abstraction. John of the Cross used epistemology only to the extent that it would help him explain his teaching. Making use of the classical theories of Aristotle and Aquinas, he sought to provide some way of understanding the kind of knowing that occurs in infused contemplation, of which, admittedly, there is comparatively speaking little firsthand knowledge.

> *I entered into unknowing*
> *and there I remained unknowing*
> *transcending all knowledge.*
>
> I entered into unknowing,
> yet when I saw myself there,
> without knowing where I was,
> I understood great things;
> I will not say what I felt
> for I remained in unknowing
> *transcending all knowledge.*
>
> That perfect knowledge
> was of peace and holiness
> held at no remove [understood directly]
> in profound solitude;
> it was something so secret
> that I was left stammering,
> *transcending all knowledge.*
>
> I was so 'whelmed,
> so absorbed and withdrawn,

that my senses were left
deprived of all their sensing,
and my spirit was given
an understanding while not understanding,
*transcending all knowledge.* (P 4.1-3)

In her inimitable way, St. Teresa also strained to speak about this paradox of mystical knowledge in which one knows but not in the way people are used to knowing. "The intellect, if it understands, doesn't understand how it understands; at least it can't comprehend anything of what it understands. It doesn't seem to me that it understands, because, as I say, it doesn't understand—I really can't understand this!" (*Life* 18.14).

With the systematic jargon of philosophy and endeavoring to explain this kind of knowledge, John gives the following account:

Because of its obscurity, she calls contemplation "night." On this account contemplation is also termed "mystical theology," meaning the secret or hidden knowledge of God. Some spiritual persons call this contemplation knowing by unknowing. For this knowledge is not produced by the intellect that the philosophers call the agent intellect, which works on the forms, phantasies, and apprehensions of the corporeal faculties; rather it is produced in the possible or passive intellect. This possible intellect, without the reception of these forms, and so on, receives passively only substantial knowledge, which is divested of images and given without any work or active function of the intellect. (C 39.12)

This text makes some weighty affirmations about the kind of knowledge experienced in contemplation. The knower is the soul, and God is the known. But it is God who reveals himself to the knower communicating a knowledge free of reliance on the senses, on words or images. No abstraction of the universal form by the agent intellect occurs. God's self-communication is nonconceptual given directly to the passive intellect. This is why John advises that in contemplation spiritual persons should remain in rest and quietude.

...even though it may seem obvious to them that they are doing nothing and wasting time, and even though they think this disinclination to think about anything is due to their laxity. Through patience and perseverance in prayer, they will be doing a great deal without activity on their part. (N 1.10.4)

If they are doing nothing, it is because activity both through the senses, with images, and through abstraction by the agent intellect is excluded. Such is the sense in which one must be quiet in prayer. In the *Living Flame of Love*, John complains of spiritual directors who mete out prosaic warnings that their directees must keep active in prayer.

How often is God anointing a contemplative soul with some very delicate unguent of loving knowledge, serene, peaceful, solitary, and far withdrawn from the senses and what is imaginable, as a result of which it cannot meditate or reflect on anything, or enjoy anything heavenly or earthly (since God has engaged it in that lonely idleness and given it the inclination to solitude), when a spiritual director will happen along who, like a blacksmith, knows no more than how to hammer and pound with the faculties. Since hammering with the faculties is this director's only teaching, and he knows no more than how to meditate, he will say: "Come, now, lay aside these rest periods, which amount to idleness and a waste of time; take and meditate and make interior acts, for it is necessary that you do your part; this other method is the way of illusions and typical of fools." (F 3.43)

## Quietism

The Spanish word for illusions (*alumbramientos*) bears the overtones of an accusation: if you aren't hammering you may be practicing the teachings of the *alumbrados*, a sect charged with illuminism or quietism. After his death, in fact, the fear did surface that John could be denounced as a quietist. For the publication of the first edition of John's writings (1618), the editor, Padre

Diego de Jesús Salablanca, went to admirable lengths to bolster the book with the best approval he could find, high recommendations from four professors of the University of Alcalá. But the *Spiritual Canticle* had to be excluded from this edition since it would have appeared too much like a disguised, vernacular commentary on the Song of Songs, something scowled upon in those times. Salablanca feared that the *alumbrados* would find shelter behind John of the Cross's teaching, thus spreading foul dust in the air and inviting the censure of the Inquisition on his works.

From the painstaking defense of John's writing by Padre Nicolás de Jesús María in 1631, we can deduce four classes of *alumbrados:* first, those who in prayer suppress all their acts, interior as well as exterior; second, those who give themselves up to a state of pure quiet, with no loving attention to God; third, those who allow their bodies to indulge every craving and maintain that, in the state of spiritual inebriation, which they have reached, they are unable to commit sin; fourth, those who consider themselves to be instruments of God, adopting the attitude of complete passivity, maintaining also that they are unable to sin because God alone is working in them. Although there may be some similarity in a few of the tenets, the teachings of John were decidedly different.

To avoid misunderstandings, Salablanca introduced hundreds of changes into John's text so that everything would sound completely orthodox. Despite this meticulous editing, the first edition of John of the Cross's writings did come under attack. Forty propositions were extracted and sent to the Inquisition for condemnation. An Augustinian professor at Salamanca, Basilio Ponce de León, wrote a distinguished and painstaking defense of the writings. He concluded his apologia with some observations that sounded more like threats. "Should the Inquisition in Spain condemn these works, there would be many well-grounded appeals made to Rome to undo what was done and make the Holy Office in Spain thereby look ridiculous." As things turned out, from what is known, the Inquisition launched no proceedings against the book. However, not for several centuries—not in fact until the first half of the twentieth century—were John's writings purged of the interpolations and omissions of the first edition and published with entire fidelity to the best manuscript copies available.

## The Will

Thought and action are distinct, and this distinction sets the stage for the discovery of a faculty that serves to connect them. Acting may follow upon thinking, but not without the intervention of a desire to translate thought into deed. Insofar as our appetites are stirred by sensation or sense images they are called "sensitive appetites." The kind of desire that depends on practical reason (the intellect that directs what it apprehends to action) may be called the "intellectual appetite" or "rational desire" or "will." Since the apparent good is the object of the appetite, the sensible good, perceived or imagined, stands to the sensitive appetite as the intelligible good, judged by reason, stands to the intellectual appetite or will. For John of the Cross, then, the will is a power of the spirit by which one wishes and chooses. Being the supreme appetite in a human being, the will alone seeks all purely spiritual or rational goods and it rejects rational and spiritual evils. It does not limit itself, however, to spiritual things; it seeks also to obtain or avoid physical goods sought by the sensitive appetites; but when the will acts in this sphere it does so because it sees reasonableness in these physical goods. One passage from John of the Cross illustrates sufficiently his conception of this spiritual faculty.

*You shall love the Lord, your God, with all your heart, and with all your soul, and with all your strength* [Deut. 6:5]. This passage contains all that spiritual persons must do and all that I must teach them here if they are to reach God by union of the will through charity. In it human beings receive the command to employ all the faculties, appetites, operations, and emotions of their soul in God so that they will use all this ability and strength for nothing else, in accord with David's words: "I will keep my strength for you" [Ps. 59:10].

The strength of the soul comprises the faculties, passions, and appetites. All this strength is ruled by the will. When the will directs these faculties, passions, and appetites toward God, turning away from all that is not God, the soul preserves its strength for God, and comes to love him with all its might.

So a person may do this, we will discuss here the purification of the will of all inordinate emotions. These inordinate emotions are the source of unruly appetites, affections, and operations, and the basis for failure to preserve one's strength for God. (A 3.16.1–2)

Because of the appetitive nature of the will, John speaks of emotions, appetites, and so on, instead of apprehensions. Since in John's system the theological virtues, each in its own area, do the work of purification, charity purifies the entire appetitive or affective dimension of a person.

### The Memory

The two faculties in relation to the two main areas of the soul's activity, cognitive and appetitive, are the only two faculties that Aquinas distinguishes. For Aquinas the intellect is said to remember only in the sense of activating an intellectual habit. He claims that if in the notion of memory we include its object as something past, then the memory is not in the intellectual, but only in the sensitive part.

Since there was a tradition, coming through the Carmelite John Baconthorpe (fourteenth century) and going back to St. Augustine, of seeing in the threefold distinction of spiritual faculties a created image of the Trinity, John added a third spiritual faculty, the memory. For him it is first and foremost a faculty of recalling and remembering, voluntary or involuntary. If memory is the activity of recalling, evoking, and welcoming apprehensions, it is also the actual capacity to keep or retain these images, forms, and experiences. The interior senses are the storehouse for all material coming through the senses.

## The Substance of the Soul

The memory can also recall apprehensions that are spiritual. Where is the storehouse for these? The memory recalls them from the common sense, not the corporeal interior common sense, but the "common sense of the spirit," the storehouse for contemplative experiences of God. This common sense of the soul is for John the deep unified center of the soul in which the faculties are rooted. He also calls it the substance of the soul. Here he follows the tradition not of philosophers but of mystics, such as Eckhart, Tauler, and Rusbroeck, when they describe the experience of mystical union as something that takes place "in the deepest part of the soul." To be sure, though, John writes out of his own experience and not simply under the influence of other sources.

The following texts provide an example of his explanation of the functioning of the spiritual faculties when they are in full union with God.

Since every living being lives by its operations, as the philosophers say, and the soul's operations are in God through its union with him, it lives the life of God. Thus it changed its death to life, its animal life to spiritual life.

The intellect, which before this union understood naturally by the vigor of its natural light, by means of the natural senses, is now moved and informed by another higher principle of supernatural divine light, and the senses are bypassed. Accordingly, the intellect becomes divine, because through its union with God's intellect both become one.

And the will, which previously loved in a base and deadly way, only with its natural affection, is now changed into the life of divine love, for it loves in a lofty way, with divine affection, moved by the strength of the Holy Spirit in which it now lives the life of love. By means of this union, God's will and the soul's will are now one.

And the memory, which by itself perceived only the figures and phantasms of creatures, is changed through this union so as to have in its mind the eternal years mentioned by David [Ps. 77:5].

And the natural appetite, which only had the ability and strength to relish creatures (which causes death), is changed now so that its taste and savor are divine, and it is moved and satisfied by another principle: the delight of God, in which it is more alive. And because it is united with him, it is no longer anything else than the appetite of God.

Finally all the movements, operations, and inclinations the soul had previously from the principle and strength of its natural life are now in this union dead to what they formerly were, changed into divine movements, and alive to God. For the soul, like a true daughter of God, is moved in all by the Spirit of God, as St. Paul teaches in saying that those who are moved by the Spirit of God are children of God himself [Rom. 8:14]. (F 2.34)

Continuing in this same passage John uses the term "substance" in its ontological sense, referring to the nature of the soul:

and although the substance of this soul is not the substance of God, since it cannot undergo a substantial conversion into him, it has become God through participation in God, being united to and absorbed in him, as it is in this state. (F 2.34)

In the next passage he uses the term "substance" in the mystical sense.

The soul says he dwells in its heart in secret because this sweet embrace is wrought in the depths of its substance. . . .

It is in the soul in which less of its own appetites and pleasures dwell where he dwells more alone, more pleased, and more as though in his own house, ruling and governing it. And he dwells more in secret, the more he dwells alone. Thus in this soul in which neither any appetite nor other images or forms nor any affections for created things dwell, the Beloved dwells secretly with an embrace so much the closer, more intimate and interior, the purer and more alone the soul is to everything other than God. His dwelling is in secret, then, because the devil cannot reach the area of this embrace, nor can the human intellect understand how it occurs.... He is usually there, in this embrace with his bride, as though asleep in the substance of the soul. And it is very well aware of him and ordinarily enjoys him. (F 4.14–15)

Although John makes ample use of the partition of the soul into faculties as principles of action, his predominant interest is a person's concrete relations with God. In the divine self-communication to our spiritual faculties in contemplation, God takes the place of a form, and enables us through this self-communication, received by us as faith, hope, and love, to enter into personal friendship with God in the divine mystery. The theological virtues are the new life for Christians, freeing them from the old self and bringing them into community with God.

# Chapter 8

# A Journey in Faith

In beginning the last chapter I pointed out that to proceed along "the way of proficients," "the way of infused contemplation," or the "illuminative way," you must walk by faith. More now must be said about this steady advancement in faith. First, it is inconceivable for John of the Cross that anyone could walk in faith without walking also in hope and love, thus making it equally possible to speak of a journey in hope or a journey in love. But John had chosen to comment on a poem he had written in which the lover escapes at night to find and be united with her beloved. Night for him here was a symbol for faith.

> One dark night,
> fired with love's urgent longings
> —ah, the sheer grace!—
> I went out unseen,
> my house being now all stilled.
>
> In darkness and secure,
> by the secret ladder, disguised,
> —ah, the sheer grace!—
> in darkness and concealment,
> my house being now all stilled.
>
> On that glad night,
> in secret, for no one saw me,
> nor did I look at anything,

with no other light or guide
than the one that burned in my heart.

This guided me
more surely than the light of noon
to where he was awaiting me
—him I knew so well—
there in a place where no one appeared.

O guiding night!
O night more lovely than the dawn!
O night that has united
the Lover with his beloved,
transforming the beloved in her Lover.

Upon my flowering breast
which I kept wholly for him alone,
there he lay sleeping,
and I caressing him
there in a breeze from the fanning cedars.

When the breeze blew from the turret,
as I parted his hair,
it wounded my neck
with its gentle hand,
suspending all my senses.

I abandoned and forgot myself,
laying my face on my Beloved;
all things ceased; I went out from myself,
leaving my cares
forgotten among the lilies. (P 2)

In commencing his commentary, John reasons that since in the night we experience darkness, which is the absence or privation of light, going out at night to seek is metaphorically going out by way of privation to seek. The notion of privation sets the negative tone for his work *The Ascent of Mount Carmel,* which starts out as a commentary on the above poem. This negative thrust presents a problem for a people steeped in the power of positive thinking. In the *Spiritual Canticle,* the journey to God is drawn in the images of an impassioned love story. The shepherdess, or bride-soul, also goes out seeking her beloved, but now not at night, for he is pasturing his sheep in the warm light of mid-day. The thrust is positive: love heals and fulfills. But in both texts, although one perspective may predominate, we find light and darkness, presence and absence.

### The Theological Life

Living by faith, hope, and love is a theological life because these virtues have God for their object. They are the living expression of union with God and all movement toward union, the heart of the Christian spiritual and mystical life. Like an axle, they support our relationships with God, with others, and with ourselves, even with our history. They constitute both the way and the goal of divine union. Although John calls them virtues, in reality he considers them to be forms of God's self-communication: transcendent truth, generous love, possession.

When speaking of the theological virtues, John has especially in mind Christians who have begun to receive contemplation. God's self-communication in contemplation creates in us the corresponding receptive capacities and attitudes of faith, hope, and love. But were we to take only the latter dimension, something would be lacking in the process. God is the substance of faith. God is love, lover, beloved.

To ascend to the flowering fields of union with God is to cut free from the briers of our entangling attachments to other objects. Reading in the *Ascent of Mount Carmel* John's detailed analysis of the climb, or escape, under the image of night as privation (privation of light), the reader incurs the risk of paying excessive attention to the objects that must be denied and not enough to the theological life that the negation demands.

We must discuss the method of leading the three faculties (intellect, memory, and will) into this spiritual night, the means to divine union. But we must first explain how the theological virtues, faith, hope, and charity (related to these faculties as their proper supernatural objects), through which the soul is united with God, cause the same emptiness and darkness in their respective faculties: faith in the intellect, hope in the memory, and charity in the will. Then we shall explain how in order to journey to God the intellect must be perfected in the darkness of faith, the memory in the emptiness of hope, and the will in the nakedness and absence of every affection.

As a result, it will be seen how necessary it is for the soul, if it is to walk securely, to journey through this dark night with the support of these three virtues. They darken and empty it of all things. As we said, the soul is not united with God in this life through understanding, or through enjoyment, or through imagination, or through any other sense; but only faith, hope, and charity (according to the intellect, memory, and will) can unite the soul with God in this life.

These virtues, as we said, void the faculties: Faith causes darkness and a void of understanding in the intellect, hope begets an emptiness of possessions in the memory, and charity produces the nakedness and emptiness of affection and joy in all that is not God.

Faith, we saw, affirms what cannot be understood by the intellect. St. Paul refers to it in Hebrews in this way: "Faith is the substance of things hoped for, the evidence of things not seen" [Heb. 11:1]. In relation to our discussion here, this means that faith is the substance of things to be hoped for and that these things are not manifest to the intellect, even though its consent to them is firm and certain. If they were manifest, there would be no faith. For though faith brings certitude to the intellect, it does not produce clarity, but only darkness.

Hope, also, undoubtedly puts the memory in darkness and emptiness as regards all earthly and heavenly objects. Hope always pertains to the unpossessed object. If something were possessed there could no longer be hope for it. St. Paul says in Romans: "Hope that is seen is not hope, for how does a person hope for what is seen—that is, what is possessed?" [Rom. 8:24]. As a result this virtue also occasions emptiness, since it is concerned with unpossessed things and not with the possessed object.

Charity, too, causes a void in the will regarding all things since it obliges us to love God above everything. We have to withdraw our affection from all in order to center it wholly upon God. Christ says through St. Luke: "Whoever does not renounce all that the will possesses cannot be my disciple" [Luke 14:33]. Consequently, these three virtues place a soul in darkness and emptiness in respect to all things. . . .

We must lead the faculties of the soul, then, to these three virtues and inform each faculty with one of them by stripping and darkening it of everything that is not conformable to these virtues. Doing this refers to the spiritual night which we above called active, because one does what lies in one's own power to enter this night. As we outlined for the sensory night a method of emptying the sense faculties, with regard to the appetite, of their visible objects, that the soul might leave the point of departure for the mean, which is faith, so for this spiritual night we will present, with the divine help, a method of emptying and purifying the spiritual faculties of all that is not God. By this method these faculties can abide in the darkness of these three virtues, which are the means and preparation, as we said, for the soul's union with God.

This method provides complete security against the cunning of the devil and the power of self-love in all its ramifications. Usually self-love subtly deceives and hinders the journey of spiritual persons along this road, because they do not know how to denude and govern themselves by means of these three virtues. They never succeed, therefore, in finding the substance and purity of spiritual good; neither do they journey by as straight and short a road as they might.

Remember that I am now especially addressing those who have begun to enter the state of contemplation. . . . (A 2.6.1–4, 6–8).

The preceding passage outlines all that John explains item by item concerning the correct attitude we must bring to contemplation as well as to all the other activities of our lives. Without this attitude we will only fumble and stumble on the road to divine union. It bears on a new stance, which is both theological and mystical. We cannot perceive God through our limited patterns of perception; we would thereby distort who God is. We may have recourse to every kind of means to go to God (ideas, images, feelings, representations), but must not get locked into their limitations or our own subjectivity.

### God's Hiding Place Is Darkness

Discussing the theological life in the *Ascent of Mount Carmel,* John creates a general air of darkness or obscurity. As intensely as he exalts the union of transformation, he insists on the objective distance between God and human beings and on the void and emptiness that we suffer as a consequence. The darkness does not come from the distance but from God's communication itself. Even after the revelation that comes to us in faith through Jesus Christ, God continues to be an unfathomable mystery for the Christian.

Sometimes God favors advanced souls, through what they hear, see, or understand—and sometimes independently of this—with a sublime knowledge by which they receive an understanding or experience of the height and grandeur of God. Their experience of God in this favor is so lofty that they understand clearly that everything remains to be understood. This understanding and experience that the divinity is so immense as to surpass complete understanding is indeed a sublime knowledge.

One of the outstanding favors God grants briefly in this life is an understanding and experience of himself so lucid and lofty that one comes to know clearly that God cannot be completely understood or experienced. This understanding is somewhat like that of the Blessed in heaven: Those who understand

God more understand more distinctly the infinitude that remains to be understood; whereas those who see less of him do not realize so clearly what remains to be seen.

I do not think anyone who has not had such experience will understand this well. But, since the soul experiencing this is aware that what she has so sublimely experienced remains beyond her understanding, she calls it "I-don't-know-what." Since it is not understandable, it is indescribable, although, as I say, one may know what the experience of it is. As a result, she says the creatures are stammering, for they do not make it completely known. (C 7.9–10)

With the journey in faith, the moment never comes for saying or thinking "Ah, I have found him."

You do very well, O soul, to seek him ever as one hidden, for you exalt God and approach very near him when you consider him higher and deeper than anything you can reach. Hence, pay no attention, neither partially nor entirely, to anything your faculties can grasp. I mean that you should never seek satisfaction in what you understand about God, but in what you do not understand about him. Never stop with loving and delighting in your understanding and experience of God, but love and delight in what you cannot understand or experience of him. Such is the way, as we said, of seeking him in faith. However surely it may seem that you find, experience, and understand God, you must, because he is inaccessible and concealed, always regard him as hidden, and serve him who is hidden in a secret way. Do not be like the many foolish ones who, in their lowly understanding of God, think that when they do not understand, taste, or experience him, he is far away and utterly concealed. The contrary belief would be truer. The less distinct is their understanding of him, the closer they approach him, since in the words of the prophet Daniel, *he made darkness his hiding place* [Ps. 18:11]. Thus in drawing near him, you will experience darkness because of the weakness of your eye.

You do well, then, at all times, in both adversity and prosperity, whether spiritual or temporal, to consider God as hidden, and call after him thus: Where have you hidden, Beloved, and left me moaning? (C 1.12)

How does John of the Cross understand faith and the way we are to respond to God in faith? In faith we have a communion between two persons by which the believer shares in the truth of the one revealing, who would otherwise remain unknown. Meditating on God's word, as his Carmelite rule prescribed, John of the Cross deepened in his conviction that God gave us everything in Christ his Word. In chapter 22 of the *Ascent,* he found the apt place to expound an essential factor in his christological thought.

If I have already told you all things in my Word, my Son, and if I have no other word, what answer or revelation can I now make that would surpass this? Fasten your eyes on him alone because in him I have spoken and revealed all and in him you will discover even more than you ask for and desire. You are making an appeal for locutions and revelations that are incomplete, but if you turn your eyes to him you will find them complete. For he is my entire locution and response, vision and revelation, which I have already spoken, answered, manifested, and revealed to you by giving him to you as a brother, companion, master, ransom, and reward. On that day when I descended on him with my Spirit on Mount Tabor proclaiming: "This is my beloved Son in whom I am well pleased, hear him" [Matt. 17:5], I gave up these methods of answering and teaching and presented them to him. Hear him because I have no more faith to reveal or truths to manifest. If I spoke before, it was to promise Christ. If they questioned me, their inquiries were related to their petitions and longings for Christ in whom they were to obtain every good, as is now explained in all the doctrine of the evangelists and apostles. (A 2.22.5)

Equating faith with Christ the Word, John presents faith from the viewpoint of its content, what the scholastics called its material object. Here the object is a subject as well, the revealer himself. Since Christ reveals everything God has to tell us, including the mystery of who the Beloved Son is who has come to live

*[handwritten margin note: ? is he saying there is no more prophecy in the Church ?]*

among us and speak to us, we know all that lies in the sweep of what God tells us. But we also know personally him who tells us. Nonetheless, we do not see God clearly on earth nor can we prove all that God tells us about the divine mysteries; faith comes through hearing.

In faith we do not see; we know in darkness. As faith is actuated in contemplation, one becomes aware of the faint presence of the revealer in darkness. With your eyes fixed on him, the revealer will become everything for you: friend, teacher, rescuer, beloved. He is himself the light by which you know him in darkness since your faith is your share in this light. In sum, contemplation is an activity of faith in which we are present to and experience the presence of Christ who is always present to us, the revealer and revelation itself.

We cannot see the glorified Jesus; in this human condition we cannot see God without dying. But we can see in faith; we can look at him, be present to him with all our being in faith, as we would be present to someone in a dark room. Thus John shows a fascination for the obscure character of faith. Faith is a "dark night," a "dark cloud," "dark water," a "blind person's guide." He noticed that whenever God communicated at length with someone, God was present in darkness. After Solomon finished the temple, God filled it with darkness; appearing to Moses on Mount Sinai, God was covered with darkness; God spoke to Job from the dark air. But there is a paradox to be dealt with: the dark cloud illumines.

How wonderful it was: A cloud, dark in itself, could illumine the night! This was related to illustrate how faith, a dark and obscure cloud to souls . . . illumines and pours light into their darkness by means of its own darkness. (A 2.3, 5)

To be more exact, we would feel urged to say that Christ is the "dark night," the "dark cloud," the "dark water," the "blind person's guide." Christ, the blinding light, is the Revealer who communicates a loving knowledge, pours the light of his truth into the receiver, who is blinded but nonetheless accepts this truth and surrenders in trust to the Revealer who cannot deceive. Our assent and surrender, then, do not arise from any understanding of the propositions of faith. These propositions are always inadequate and incomplete—even though correct—statements about the Christian faith, about the trinitarian God and the participation Christians may have through Christ in the life of God.

To bring the intellect into submission, a person must make an act of free choice. When Christ communicates the light of faith, which is himself, the recipient is mysteriously drawn to him as to a friend. Love is indispensable in the life of faith. God's activity in Jesus Christ cannot be accepted first of all by the intellect (in belief) in order to elicit then a corresponding return of love.

Faith receives the mystery and becomes certain of it in the degree to which it affirms the mystery in love. But in all the truths of love, the contemplative perceives the presence of the Beloved.

She calls these truths "eyes" because of the remarkable presence of the Beloved she experiences. It seems that he is now always looking at her. (C 12.5)

In the contemplative gaze of faith, two lovers are present to each other. Christ is fully present; the contemplative is present according to the measure of love.

## Visions and Locutions

There is a way of knowing and a kind of knowledge not yet mentioned of which John is sternly skeptical: the particular knowledge that comes not through our own efforts but passively either as vision or locution. This knowledge, which John also classifies as supernatural, it being passive, cannot serve as a proximate means to union with God as does faith. But it will stand like a barricade of stone on the path to union with God.

I say, then, that since these imaginative apprehensions, visions, and other forms or species are presented through some image or particular idea, individuals should neither feed upon nor encumber themselves with them. And this is true whether these visions be false and diabolical or whether they be recognized as authentic and from God. Neither should people desire to accept them or keep them. Thus they can remain detached, divested, pure, simple, and without any mode or method as the union demands.

The reason is that in being apprehended these forms are always represented . . . in some limited mode or manner. But God's wisdom, to which the intellect must be united, has neither mode nor manner, neither does it have limits nor does it pertain to distinct and particular knowledge, because it is totally pure and simple. That the two extremes, the soul and the divine Wisdom, may be united, they will have to come to accord by means of a certain likeness. As a result the soul must also be pure and simple, unlimited and unattached to any particular knowledge, and unmodified by the boundaries of form, species, and image. Since God cannot be encompassed by any image, form, or particular knowledge, the soul in order to be united with him should not be limited by any particular form or knowledge.

The Holy Spirit in Deuteronomy clearly manifests that God has no form or likeness: "You heard the voice of his words, and you saw absolutely no form in God" [Deut. 4:12]. But he affirms that darkness, the cloud, and obscurity (that vague, dark knowledge, we mentioned, in which the soul is united to God) were present. . . .

To reach this essential union of love of God, a person must be careful not to lean upon imaginative visions, forms, figures, or particular ideas, since they cannot serve as a proportionate and proximate means for such an effect; instead, they would be a hindrance. As a result a person should renounce them and endeavor to avoid them. The only reason for admitting and valuing them would be the profit and good effect the genuine ones bring to the soul. But admitting them is unnecessary to obtain this good effect; for the sake of progress, rather, one should always deny them. . . .

One cannot advance in faith without closing one's eyes to everything pertaining to the senses and to clear, particular knowledge. Though St. Peter was truly certain of his vision of Christ's glory in the transfiguration, yet after relating the fact in his second canonical epistle [2 Pet. 1:16-18], he did not want anyone to take this as the chief testimony for certitude. But leading them on to faith he declared: ... We have a more certain testimony than this vision of Tabor: the sayings and words of the prophets bearing testimony to Christ which you must make good use of, as a candle shining in a dark place [2 Pet. 1:19].

Reflecting on this comparison, we discover the doctrine we are teaching here. Telling us to behold the faith spoken of by the prophets as we would a candle shining in a dark place, he asserts that we should live in darkness, with our eyes closed to all other lights, and that in this darkness faith alone—which is dark also—should be the light we use. If we want to employ these other bright lights of distinct knowledge, we cease to make use of faith, the dark light, and we cease to be enlightened in the dark place mentioned by St. Peter. This place (the intellect—the holder on which the candle of faith is placed) must remain in darkness until the day, in the next life, when the clear vision of God dawns upon the soul; and in this life, until the daybreak of transformation in and union with God, the goal of a person's journey. (A 2.16.3-15)

### In the Community of Faith

No one walks alone who walks by faith. Where loving faith increases, rough individualism decreases. Without human counsel and guidance the person of faith remains dissatisfied. It may come as a surprise that after all that was said about faith, John should give such sweeping approval of reason. He firmly believes that "to declare and strengthen truth on the basis of natural reason, God draws near those who come together in an endeavor to know it" (A 2.22.11).

Christian mystics, then, never reach a height, however elevated, in which they get beyond the community of the church.

"We must be guided humanly and visibly in all by the law of Christ, who is human, and that of his Church and of his ministers" (A 22.7). The norm is that "God will not bring clarification and confirmation of the truth to the heart of one who is alone" (A 2.22.11). It is amazing that Paul after his exalted revelations of Christ had to go and consult with Peter. Even when a revelation is authentically from God, there are still many aspects of it and related matters that we can understand only within the faith community of the church and through our reasoning powers. John firmly asserts that all matters must be regulated by reason save those of faith, which transcend but are not contrary to reason. We received the faith from those who believed before us, and in faith we are supported by the whole community of believers. One always believes in and with the church.

Our wayfaring in faith does not free us from getting lost in a labyrinth of difficulties, needs, and tests. Our fragilely bound society can blunder and the community stumble into a muddle, not knowing or agreeing on where to turn. Here is when a clear revelation from above would help. But John says no, we must not look for answers from shadowy private revelations. What must we do, then, if despite many efforts of the reasonable mind we find no satisfying solution to our problem? John teaches that we must still remain within the boundaries of faith and there wait and pray and hope for God to provide by the means he desires.

We should make such use of reason and the law of the gospel that, even though—whether we desire it or not—some supernatural truths are told to us, we accept only what is in harmony with reason and the gospel law. And then we should receive this truth, not because it is privately revealed to us, but because it is reasonable, and we should brush aside all feelings about the revelation. We ought, in fact, to consider and examine the reasonableness of the truth when it is revealed even more than when it is not since the devil in order to delude souls says much that is true, conformed to reason, and that will come to pass.

In all our necessities, trials, and difficulties, no better or safer aid exists for us than prayer and hope that God will provide for us by the means he desires. Scripture counsels this where we read that King Jehoshaphat, deeply afflicted and surrounded by his enemies [2 Chron. 20:1-4], began to pray to God:... "When means are lacking and reason cannot find a way of providing for our necessities, we have only to raise our eyes to you that you may provide in the manner most pleasing to you" [2 Chron. 20:12]. (A 2.21.4-5)

# Chapter 9

# Absorbed in the Supreme Good

The more that individuals desire darkness and annihilation of themselves regarding all visions, exteriorly or interiorly receivable, the greater will be the infusion of faith and consequently of love and hope, since these three theological virtues increase together.

But a person does not always grasp or feel this love, because it does not reside with tenderness in the senses, but resides in the soul with properties of strength and of greater courage and daring than before, though at times it overflows into the senses imparting a gentle, tender feeling. (A 2.24.8–9)

All the senses and faculties generally interact and do so interdependently. John asserts this fact from different standpoints and with various concrete applications. According to him, the appetites increase and weaken together; the vices grow when any one of them does; the passions are conditioned and modified by one another; the spiritual faculties are purified separately and simultaneously; the virtues increase and grow perfect in the exercise of one of them.

## The Memory

The forces that can move and orient the memory's activity of recalling are the will (A 3.13.1), the devil (A 3.4.2), and God (C 35.5)—and even the pressure of the unconscious (N 1.4.4). The memory is an activity of recalling, evoking, and welcoming apprehensions. It is also the capacity to keep or retain these images, forms, and experiences. In this way the memory can be said to possess. It possesses actual memories that by virtue of the function of recalling emerge into consciousness. Memory is a capacity that can be filled; by that very fact, it can be emptied. But the word "capacity" can lend itself to confusion. A spiritual faculty is not a storage place. The memory is a capacity in the sense that it possesses the ability to focus its attention on one or several memories at the same time and hold them in the field of consciousness. The memory can empty itself completely; yet the memories are not lost, because they are conserved outside of this faculty, as mentioned in chapter 7.

This is our task now with the memory. We must draw it away from its natural props and boundaries and raise it above itself (above all distinct knowledge and apprehensible possession) to supreme hope for the incomprehensible God.

To begin with natural knowledge in the memory, I include under this heading all that can be formed from the objects of the five corporeal senses (hearing, sight, smell, taste, and touch), and everything like this sensory knowledge that the memory can evoke and fashion. It must strip and empty itself of all this knowledge and these forms and strive to lose the imaginative apprehension of them. It should do this in such a way that no knowledge or trace of them remains in it; rather it should be bare and clear, as though nothing passed through it, forgetful of all and suspended.

There is no way to union with God without annihilating the memory as to all forms. This union cannot be wrought without a complete separation of the memory from all forms that are not God.... God cannot be encompassed by any form or distinct knowledge. Since, as Christ affirms, no one can serve two masters [Matt. 6:24], and since the memory cannot at the same time be united with God and with forms and distinct knowledge, and since God has no form or image comprehensible to the memory, the memory is without form and without figure, when united with God. Its imagination being lost, in great forgetfulness, without the remembrance of anything, it is absorbed in a supreme good. This is noted every day through experience. That divine union empties and sweeps the phantasy of all forms and knowledge, and elevates it to the supernatural. (A 3.2.3–4)

Here we have a description of the situation of the memory during unitive contemplation, in which the soul is completely recollected in God without any maundering of the mind.

John calls the memories "apprehensions of the memory" and divides them according to their objects into three kinds: natural apprehensions (knowledge of objects perceived through the senses), supernatural imaginative apprehensions (visions, revelations, locutions, and spiritual feelings), and the supernatural spiritual apprehensions (touches and feelings of union with God). The natural, supernatural imaginative, and spiritual apprehensions (which do not concern the Creator) must be set aside.

John does make the concession, however, that a person may recall supernatural apprehensions when this is done on the grounds that they inspire love and for the sake of that love.

In these apprehensions coming from above (imaginative or any other kind—it matters not if they be visions, locutions, spiritual feelings, or revelations), individuals should only advert to the love of God that is interiorly caused. They should pay no attention to the letter and rind (what is signified, represented, or made known). Thus they should pay heed not to the feelings of delight or sweetness, not to the images, but to the feelings of love that are caused.

Only for the sake of moving the spirit to love should the soul at times recall the images and apprehensions that produced love. Though the effect produced by the remembrance of this communication is not as strong as at the time the communication was received, yet, when the communication is recalled, there is a renewal of love and an elevation of the mind to God. This is especially true when the soul remembers some figures, images, or supernatural feelings. These are usually so imprinted on it that they last a long time; some are never erased from the soul. These apprehensions produce, almost as often as remembered, divine effects of love, sweetness, light, and so on—sometimes in a greater degree, sometimes in a lesser—because God impressed them for this reason. This is consequently a great grace, for those on whom God bestows it possess within themselves a mine of blessings.

The figures producing such effects are vividly impressed on the soul, for they are not like other images and forms preserved in the phantasy. The soul has no need of recourse to this faculty when it desires to remember them, for it is aware that it has them within itself as an image in a mirror. When a soul possesses these figures formally within itself, it can safely recall them for the procuring of the effect of love I mentioned. They will not be a hindrance to the union of love in faith providing the soul is undesirous of being absorbed with the figure. It must profit from the love by immediately leaving aside the figure. In this way the remembrance will instead be a help to the soul.

It is difficult to discern when these images are impressed on the soul and when on the phantasy. For those of the phantasy are also quite frequent. Some persons who usually have imaginative visions find that these same visions are very frequently represented in their phantasy, either because they themselves possess a very lively faculty, so that with little thought the ordinary figure is immediately represented and sketched on it, or because the devil causes these representations, or also because God causes them without impressing them formally in the soul.

Nonetheless they can be discerned through their effects. For those that are of natural or diabolical origin produce no good effect or spiritual renewal in the soul, no matter how often they are remembered. The individual beholds them in dryness. When remembered, however, the imaginative apprehensions from God produce some good effect by means of that which they imparted to the soul the first time. Yet the formal apprehensions—those impressed on the soul—yield some effect almost every time they are recalled.

Anyone with the experience of these will easily be able to

tell the difference between the two, for the diversity between them is very clear. I merely assert that those impressed formally on the soul in a lasting way are of rarer occurrence. But whatever may be their kind, it is good for the soul to have no desire to comprehend anything save God alone in hope through faith.

As for the other point in the objection (that it is apparently pride to reject these apprehensions if they are good), I answer: Rather, it is prudent humility to benefit by them in the best way, as has been mentioned, and be guided along the safest path. (A 3.13.6–9)

St. Teresa of Avila's fruitful visions of Christ were of two kinds, intellectual and imaginative, and often included both simultaneously; in John's language that means that the apprehensions were often impressed on the soul and represented as well in the phantasy. She insisted, and John of the Cross here would not object, that the effort to dismiss Christ from one's prayer lest he be an obstacle to some higher union with the Godhead would be an egregious error and would actually impede further progress.

The category called "spiritual apprehensions of God" is the final one. These do not have a corporeal image and form and therefore present no problem by their being retained in the memory.

But as for knowledge of the Creator, I declare that a person should strive to remember it as often as possible because it will produce in the soul a notable effect. For... the communications of this knowledge are touches and spiritual feelings of union with God, the goal to which we are guiding the soul. The memory does not recall these through any form, image, or figure that may have been impressed on the soul, for those touches and feelings of union with the Creator do not have any. It remembers them through the effect of light, love, delight, spiritual renewal, and so on, produced in it. Something of this effect is renewed as often as the soul recalls them. (A 3.14.2)

The spiritual faculties deposit what is communicated to them during the union in the "common sense of the soul," mentioned in chapter 7, which is the receptacle or archives.

By the "feeling" of the soul, the verse refers to the power and strength that the substance of the soul has for feeling and enjoying the objects of the spiritual faculties; through these faculties a person tastes the wisdom and love and communication of God. The soul here calls these three faculties (memory, intellect, and will) "the deep caverns of feeling" because through them and in them it deeply experiences and enjoys the grandeurs of God's wisdom and excellence.... All these things are received and seated in this feeling of the soul which, as I say, is its power and capacity for experiencing, possessing, and tasting them all. And the caverns of the faculties administer them to it, just as the bodily senses go to assist the common sense of the phantasy with the forms of their objects, and this common sense becomes the receptacle and archives of these forms. Hence this common sense, or feeling, of the soul, which has become the receptacle or archives of God's grandeurs, is illumined and enriched according to what it attains of this high and enlightened possession. (F 3.69)

Memories are not destroyed through the process of purification, nor can we erase them; but all is renewed, thereby effecting the new harmony that results in our passage from the old self to the new. Even the old, unpleasant secrets of sin may serve a purpose in their recall.

Yet even though God forgets evil and sin once it is pardoned, the soul should not become oblivious of her former sins. As the Wise Man says: *Be not without fear for sin forgiven* [Ecclus. 5:5]. There are three reasons why she should not forget her sins: first, so as always to have a motive against presumption; second, to have cause for rendering thanks; third, to incite herself to greater confidence, for if while in sin the soul received so much good from God, how many more remarkable favors will she be able to hope for now that God has placed her in his love, outside of sin? (C 33.1)

## Theological Hope

It is the theological virtue of hope (distinct from the emotion of hope) that empties the memory of possessions so that the concern of the soul will center only on God. The theological life consists of a new manner of knowing, remembering, and loving. It is the colorful disguise in which the soul daringly escapes at night unrecognized by its old enemies (the world, the flesh, and the devil). It consists of a white tunic (faith), a green coat of mail (hope), and a red toga (charity).

As a result, this green livery, by which one always gazes on God, looks at nothing else, and is not content save with him alone, so pleases the Beloved that it is true to say the soul obtains from God all that she hopes for from him. The Bridegroom of the Canticle consequently says of his bride that she wounded his heart by merely the look of her eyes [Song 4:9]. Without this green livery of hope in God alone, it would not behoove anyone to go out toward this goal of love; a person would obtain nothing, since what moves and conquers is unrelenting hope.

The soul advances through this dark and secret night in the disguise of the green livery of hope, for she walks along so empty of all possession and support that neither her eyes nor her care are taken up with anything but God. (N 2.21.8–9)

John identified faith with Christ; so too hope in its own way is Christ. The Bridegroom Christ is the object, the one whom we must hope to possess:

There is reason for you to be elated and joyful in seeing that all your good and hope is so close as to be within you, or better, that you cannot be without him. (C 1.7)

In concluding his short section on the purification of the memory through hope, John sums up the work of hope for us.

The following must be kept in mind: Our aim is union with God in the memory through hope; the object of hope is something unpossessed; the less other objects are possessed, the more capacity and ability there is to hope for this one object, and consequently the more hope; the greater the possessions, the less capacity and ability for hoping, and consequently so much less of hope; accordingly, in the measure that individuals dispossess their memory of forms and objects, which are not God, they will fix it on God and preserve it empty, so as to hope for the fullness of their memory from him. That which souls must do in order to live in perfect and pure hope in God is this: As often as distinct ideas, forms, and images occur to them, they should immediately, without resting in them, turn to God with loving affection, in emptiness of everything rememberable. (A 3.15.1)

To be empty is to be detached from all else but God, and the way to do this is to turn away from the things occupying our minds, turning instead to God with loving affection and desire for him. Throughout the *Ascent of Mount Carmel*, John teaches with much detail this practice of loving attention to God. The "loving" part of the attention (in faith) embraces the desire or hope for God.

But we have to live in the world, a world hectic with activities, weighted down in its vast sweep with jobs, duties, and commitments. Admittedly, and phrasing it mildly, John did not dwell on such matters as much as he did on the necessity of emptying our intellects and memories of all apprehensions in order to go to God. But he does not neglect to set forth two important principles that are needed here, and he leaves it up to his readers to apply them.

They should not think or look on these things [memories and other ideas] for longer than is sufficient for the understanding and fulfillment of their obligations, if these refer to this. And then they should consider these ideas without becoming attached or seeking gratification in them, lest the effects of them be left in the soul. Thus people are not required to stop recalling and thinking about what they must do and know, for, if they are not attached to the possession of these thoughts, they will not be harmed. (A 3.15.1)

What harm can be done to us by our memories? Through them we fall victim to many illusions, wild feelings, unbid cravings, rash judgments, and a poor use of time. Regarding John's analyses, we can limit our focus here to the disturbance these memories cause to the peace that supports contemplative prayer and recollection.

To explain how these apprehensions are a hindrance to moral good, one must know that moral good consists in bridling the passions and curbing the inordinate appetites. The result for the soul is tranquility, peace, repose, and moral virtue, which is the moral good.

The soul is incapable of truly acquiring control of the passions and restriction of the inordinate appetites without forgetting and withdrawing from the sources of these emotions. Disturbances never arise in a soul unless through the apprehensions of the memory. When all things are forgotten, nothing disturbs the peace or stirs the appetites. As the saying goes: What the eye doesn't see, the heart doesn't want.

We have experience of this all the time. We observe that as often as people begin to think about some matter, they are moved and aroused over it, little or much, according to the kind of apprehension. If the apprehension is bothersome and annoying, they feel sadness or hatred, and so on; if agreeable, they will experience desire and joy, and so on.

Accordingly, when the apprehension is changed, agitation necessarily results. Thus they will sometimes be joyful, at other times sad, now they will feel hatred, now love. And they are unable to persevere in equanimity, the effect of moral tranquility, unless they endeavor to forget all things. Evidently, then, this knowledge is a serious impediment to the possession of the moral virtues.

That an encumbered memory is also a hindrance to the possession of spiritual good is clearly proved from our remarks. An unsettled soul, which has no foundation of moral good, is incapable, as such, of receiving spiritual good. For this spiritual good is impressed only on a restrained and peaceful soul.

Besides, if souls bestow importance and attention on the

apprehensions of the memory, they will find it impossible to remain free for the Incomprehensible who is God, for they will be unable to advert to more than one thing. As we have always been insisting, souls must go to God by not comprehending rather than by comprehending, and they must exchange the mutable and comprehensible for the Immutable and Incomprehensible. (A 3.5.1–3)

## The Will and the Emotions

The teachings, advice, and warnings to direct the intellect and memory in faith and hope could not be complied with apart from the will (the desire or appetite as determined by reason). All pleasures and attachments are caused by things that appear good and delightful to a person. So the will as an appetite moves toward these objects with emotion. John employs the terms "passions" and "affections" for what we may more commonly call emotions. Passion is now usually restricted to the more vehement aspect of any emotional experience. But anyone open to ideas from many centuries can use these terms interchangeably. Emotional experience seems to involve an awareness of widespread bodily commotion, which includes changes in the tension of the blood vessels and the muscles, changes in heartbeat, breathing, and so on. Though some degree of bodily disturbance would seem to be an essential ingredient in all emotional experience, the intensity and extent of the physiological reverberation, or bodily commotion, is not the same or equal in all the emotions.

Like desire, emotion is neither knowledge nor action, but something intermediate between the one and the other. The various passions are usually aroused by objects perceived, imagined, or remembered, and once aroused they in turn originate impulses to act in certain ways. John borrowed from Boethius the reduction of the classical eleven passions of Aristotle to four (joy, hope, fear, and sorrow). Thus he states in a letter:

All pleasures, joys, and attachments are ever caused in the soul by means of the desire and will for things that appear good, suitable, and delightful, being in the soul's opinion satisfying and precious. And accordingly the appetite of the will moves toward these things, hopes for them, rejoices in their possession, fears their loss, and grieves on losing them. And thus, according to its attachments and joy in things, the soul is disturbed and restless. (L 13)

In dealing with the purification of the intellect and memory, John had to treat of the apprehensions of these faculties. But in dealing with the appetitive faculty, he must speak not of apprehensions but of passions, appetites, and affections. These emotions can take command of the will and carry it off with them—and the other faculties along with it. The will is susceptible to being taken prisoner by its emotions. If this happens, the peace necessary for contemplation is obliterated. One can be in the most tranquil surroundings, but if the emotions do not remain under the rule of the will, there can be no peace.

## Theological Love

It is because they have the light of faith, in which they hope for eternal life and without which nothing from above or below will have any value, that Christians ought to direct their faculties, passions, and appetites to God, and turn away from all that is not God; that is John's teaching about purifying the will through charity.

For a treatise on the active night and denudation of this faculty, with the aim of forming and perfecting it in this virtue of the charity of God, I have found no more appropriate passage than the one in chapter 6 of Deuteronomy, where Moses commands: "You shall love the Lord, your God, with all your heart, and with all your soul, and with all your strength" [Deut. 6:5]. This passage contains all that spiritual persons must do and all that I must teach them here if they are to reach God by union of the will through charity. In it human beings receive the command to employ all the faculties, appetites, operations, and emotions of their soul in God so that they will use all this ability and strength for nothing else, in accord with David's words: "I will keep my strength for you" [Ps. 59:10]. (A 3.16.1)

The emotions are inordinate when they are not directed to God, becoming then the source of fractious appetites, affections, and activities. What John sets out to do in his treatise on the purification of the will through charity is to explain how a person must rule over the emotions and direct them to God. Ruling over them is not the equivalent in any way of repressing them. By redirecting the emotions, one can experience them in relation to God. The principle John draws from faith is that what ought to stir the emotions is whatever gives glory and honor to God or subtracts from that honor and glory. Having had the Jesuits as his teachers in his youth, he surely must have learned from them the ideal of their founder, Ignatius of Loyola: *Ad majorem dei gloriam* (For the Greater Glory of God).

But in Scripture, John's fundamental source, the glory of God deals with two related themes: the glory of God as the divine perfection and as the divine praise. In the Bible God's glory, his sublime, lordly, radiant splendor is precisely what for all eternity distinguishes him from everything else. This is his wholly otherness. In a biblical sense this means that the deeper a creature is allowed to encounter God's glory the more this creature will long to extol this glory as being exalted over itself and over all creation. When confronted by the appearance of God's glory, Moses fell to his knees and bowed his face toward the earth, Elijah hid his face in his cloak, Isaiah thought he was doomed, Ezekiel fell with his face to the ground, Daniel felt anguish of spirit and sank in a faint with his face to the earth, the apostles on Tabor were overcome with awe and in great fear fell into a sleep at the sight of it, Paul was thrown to the ground and blinded, and John fell as though dead at the feet of the appearing Lord. In the presence of God's glory, the ways of the old self are overwhelmed and annihilated and one's center shifts to God. What these biblical figures experienced so dramatically will usually only gradually be burned into the hearts of those committed to the theological life. The form, the light of Christ's life will drive off the ways of sin.

Even when God seems absent and the spirit lives in cold darkness as a result of purgative contemplation, God's glory perceived in this dark absence inexorably works its effect:

God gives from the outset an esteeming love by which he is held in such high favor that, as we said, the soul's greatest suffering in the trials of this night is the anguish of thinking it has lost God and been abandoned by him.... Their love of esteem for God is so intense, even though obscure and imperceptible, that they would be happy not only to suffer these things but even to die many times in order to please him. (N 2.13.5)

As was noted in chapter 3, the one who pleases God is the one who out of love seeks to become like the divine Son, who is the reflection of the Father's glory.

Love effects a likeness between the lover and the loved (A 1.4.3). ... In his [Jesus'] life he had no other gratification, nor desired any other, than the fulfillment of his Father's will. (A 13.4)

In the use of all our abilities and talents and the created objects of this world, the focus, then, ought to be the fulfillment of the Father's will, the glorification of God on earth, a life for the service and honor of God. The old self will work untiringly for its own pleasure, prestige, and power through these abilities and talents and for these reasons will long to possess money, intelligence, and beauty, or even spiritual consolations. Its joys will center on possessions like these.

The sign that one is shifting one's center from self and its interests to Christ and his interests can be discerned through the emotional experience that follows loss or gain. If a bequest that I had expected from a relative of mine were left instead for the church's charitable works, would I rejoice that God and the poor were being served in this way or be sad, or even angry, that I didn't receive the inheritance, which I could have used for my own interests? The intensity of the emotion will usually reveal the degree of attachment.

For there can be no voluntary joy over creatures without voluntary possessiveness, just as there can be no joy, insofar as it is a passion, unaccompanied by habitual possessiveness of

heart. The denial and purgation of such joy leaves the judgment as clear as the air when vapors vanish.

Those, then, whose joy is unpossessive of things rejoice in
them all as though they possessed them all; those others,
beholding them with a possessive mind, lose all the delight of
them all in general. The former, as St. Paul states, though they
have nothing in their heart, possess everything with greater liberty [2 Cor. 6:10]; the others, insofar as they possess things
with attachment, neither have nor possess anything. Rather,
their heart is held by things and they suffer as a captive. As
many as are the joys they long to uncover in creatures, so
many will necessarily be the straits and afflictions of their
attached and possessed heart.

Cares do not molest the detached, neither in prayer nor outside of it, and thus, losing no time, such people easily store
up an abundance of spiritual good. Yet those who are attached
spend all their time going to and fro about the snare to which
their heart is tied, and even with effort they can hardly free
themselves for a short while from this snare of thinking about
and finding joy in the object to which their heart is attached.
(A 3.20.2–3)

This detachment is the work of love. Christ's disciple does
everything with a mind to God, that is, has eyes only for God, is
always looking at God. The lover beholds the beloved uninter-
ruptedly, thinks only of him and is wholly turned toward him.
All her thinking, speaking, and acting occur solely in connection
with God. The Scriptures urge devoted followers of Christ to
praise God's glory not only in prayer but in all that they do. This
loving doxology is the animating power of the right use of all
one's emotions.

There are four of these emotions or passions: joy, hope, sorrow, and fear. These passions manifestly keep the strength and
ability of the soul for God, and direct it toward him, when they
are so ruled that a person rejoices only in what is purely for
God's honor and glory, hopes for nothing else, feels sorrow
only about matters pertaining to this, and fears only God. The

more people rejoice over something outside God, the less intense will be their joy in God; and the more their hope goes out toward something else, the less there is of it for God; and so on with the others.

To give a complete doctrine on this subject, we will, as is our custom, discuss individually these four passions as well as the appetites of the will. The entire matter of reaching union with God consists in purging the will of its appetites and emotions so that from a human and lowly will it may be changed into the divine will, made identical with the will of God.

The less strongly the will is fixed on God and the more dependent it is on creatures, the more these four passions combat the soul and reign in it. A person then very easily rejoices in what deserves no rejoicing, hopes for what brings no profit, sorrows over what should perhaps cause rejoicing, and fears where there is no reason for fear.

When these emotions go unbridled, they are the source of all vices and imperfections; but when they are put in order and calmed, they give rise to all the virtues.

It should be known that, in the measure that one of the passions is regulated according to reason, the others are also. These four passions are so interlinked and fraternal that where one goes actually the others go virtually. If one is recollected actually, the other three in the same measure are recollected virtually. If the will rejoices over something, it must consequently in the same degree hope for it, with the virtual inclusion of sorrow and fear. And in the measure that it loses satisfaction in this object, fear, sorrow, and hope will also be lost. . . .

Accordingly, you should keep in mind that wherever one of these passions goes the entire soul (the will and the other faculties) will also go, and they will live as prisoners of this passion; and the other three passions will be alive in the one so as to afflict the soul with their chains and prevent it from soaring to the liberty and repose of sweet contemplation and union. (A 3.16.2)

Ancient, medieval, and modern thinkers did not underestimate the force of the passions, nor were they too confident of the strength of reason and the will to control them, or to be free of them. But not until Freud do we find insight into the pathology of the passions, the origin of emotional disorders, and the general theory of the neuroses and neurotic character as the consequence of emotional repression.

For Freud, the primary fact is not the conflict between reason and emotion or, in his language, between the *ego* and the *id*. It is rather the repression that results from such conflict. His great insight is that emotions when repressed do not atrophy and disappear. On the contrary, their dammed-up energies accumulate and, like a sore, fester inwardly.

Whatever one may think of the whole of Freud's theories, it is worth insisting that John of the Cross's teaching not be misinterpreted in favor of the repression of the emotions. He never wants us to ignore our emotions or try to live without feelings. Nor does he hold the kindred idea that we can simply control our feelings through sheer willpower. What is needed is the love of God. The theological virtue of love purifies the soul, calming the tempest by drawing, directing, and ordering the emotions to God, to God's honor and glory. Through perseverance in prayer, the heart with its affectionate love is little by little set more entirely on the Beloved who is Christ, the content of faith, the health of the soul.

Love of God is the soul's health, and the soul does not have full health until love is complete. Sickness is nothing but the lack of health, and when the soul has not even a single degree of love, she is dead. But when she possesses some degrees of love of God, no matter how few, she is then alive, yet very weak and infirm because of her little love. In the measure that love increases she will be healthier, and when love is perfect she will have full health.

It should be known that love never reaches perfection until the lovers are so alike that one is transfigured in the other. And then the love is in full health. (C 11.11)

Since the palate of the soul's will has tasted this food of love of God, her will is inclined immediately to seek and enjoy her Beloved in everything that happens and in all her occupations without looking for any satisfaction of her own. (C 10.1)

Besides the emotions surging out of the appetites for temporal, natural, and sensory goods (with which I dealt in chapter 2), John's remaining classifications of goods are moral, supernatural (the charismatic gifts), and delightful spiritual goods (statues, religious paintings, oratories, dedicated places of prayer, ceremonies, and sermons). He could have gone on with many more kinds of goods but the *Ascent* ends abruptly.

I will choose just one class of goods for an example here, one that would seem a most unlikely source of trouble: the moral goods. Moral goods include the virtues and the works of mercy, observance of God's laws, and the practice of prudence and good manners—all those qualities we regard so highly in others. But finding our joy in these goods leads to trouble also, especially disunity, for humans like to object to religious and spiritual practices and ideas that are unconformed to their own.

There is so much misery among human beings as regards this kind of harm that I believe most of the works publicly achieved are either faulty, worthless, or imperfect in God's sight. The reason is that people are not detached from these human respects and interests.

Some want praise for their works; others, thanks; others talk about them and are pleased if this person or that or even the whole world knows about them. (A 3.28.5.) . . .

Though Christians ought to rejoice in the moral goods and works they perform temporally, insofar as these are the cause of the temporal goods we spoke of, they ought not stop there as did the gentiles, who with the eyes of their soul did not go beyond the things of this mortal life. Since Christians have the light of faith, in which they hope for eternal life, and without which nothing from above or below will have any value, they ought to rejoice in the possession and exercise of these moral goods only and chiefly in the second manner: that insofar as they perform these works for the love of God, these works procure eternal life for them.

Thus, through their good customs and virtues they should fix their eyes only on the service and honor of God....

For the sake of directing their joy in moral goods to God, Christians should keep in mind that the value of their good works, fasts, alms, penances, and so on, is not based on quantity and quality so much as on the love of God practiced in them; and consequently that these works are of greater excellence in the measure both that the love of God by which they are performed is more pure and entire and that self-interest diminishes with respect to pleasure, comfort, praise, and earthly or heavenly joy. They should not set their heart on the pleasure, comfort, savor, and other elements of self-interest these good works and practices usually entail, but recollect their joy in God and desire to serve him through these means. And through purgation and darkness as to this joy in moral goods they should in secret desire that only God be pleased and joyful over their works. They should have no other interest or satisfaction than the honor and glory of God. Thus all the strength of their will in regard to these moral goods will be recollected in God. (A 3.27.4–5)

In John's theological asceticism a genuine communion is created, not between the receiver and the gift but between the receiver and the giver. The small gift offered to God must be offered without attention to what is given, its worth, or the effort that it costs. A person should seek only for God to rejoice in the love of which the gift is an expression. The same rule holds for the gifts God gives. A person should not endeavor to obtain or rest in the gift, but aim to go beyond the gift to the Beloved who gives the gift.

The theological virtues do not stand at the margin of our subjectivity. They can incorporate all kinds of means while at the same time making them relative, urging the Christian toward communion with the living God, which is distinct from these means. They make use of the good things that mediate God's self-communication, they conserve them, and they also transcend them moving into personal communion with the Beloved.

# Chapter 10

# The Constricted Road

*Faith*
*Hope*
*Charity*

The theological virtues thread their way through all means to communion with God. Theological asceticism is the journey to the summit of Mount Carmel, the path that all Christians can and must take if they are going to follow Christ to full transformation in him.

We ought to note carefully the words our Savior spoke in St. Matthew's Gospel, chapter 7, about this road: "How narrow is the gate and constricted the way that leads to life! And few there are who find it" [Matt. 7:14]. . . . We must also note that first he says the gate is narrow to teach that entrance through this gate of Christ (the beginning of the journey) involves a divestment and narrowing of the will in relation to all sensible and temporal objects by loving God more than all of them. This task belongs to the night of sense, as we have said.

Next he asserts that the way (that is, of perfection) is constricted in order to teach that the journey along this way involves not only entering through the narrow gate, a void of sense objects, but also a constricting of oneself through dispossession and the removal of obstacles in matters relating to the spiritual part of the soul.

We can apply, then, what Christ says about the narrow gate to the sensitive part of the human person, and what he says about the constricted way to the spiritual or rational part. Since he proclaims that few find it, we ought to note the cause: Few there are with the knowledge and desire to enter into this supreme nakedness and emptiness of spirit. As this path on

173

the high mount of perfection is narrow and steep, it demands travelers who are neither weighed down by the lower part of their nature nor burdened in the higher part. This is a venture in which God alone is sought and gained, thus only God ought to be sought and gained. (A 2.7.2–3)

The need for denial through the theological life embraces both following Christ as response to his word and sharing in the mystery of his death on the cross as response to his deed. A number of important topics in the study of spirituality (for example, liturgy, the sacraments, works of charity in service of others), receive scant attention in John's writings. His readers are left to construct what he might have said from the doctrine that he did develop. Since much had already been written on such subjects, John's main intention in expounding on the ascent of Mount Carmel and the dark night was to assist travelers who feel lost and discouraged in the extreme emptiness, nakedness, and poverty of the journey in faith.

### Light, Word, and Presence

Even though Christ is the content of faith, the beloved Word and full revelation of the Father, there is a paradox about his revelation. When the light shines, it shines in darkness. Contemplation is a ray of darkness, received in darkness as the eye is blinded to all other lights. Putting the paradox in another form, he says that the Father speaks his Word in silence, and the Word can only be heard in silence. Again, in another paradox: the Word, the Beloved, dwells so close as to be within us, but is hidden there. These figures, light in darkness, Word spoken in silence, someone present yet hidden, tell of God's transcendence and that Christ in our contemplation leads us into the vast obscurity of divine transcendent mystery. The immense, boundless light of God overwhelms the limited human eye, forcing it to close. The term of the journey is darkness, or silence, or the hidden beloved.

Blinding our intellects, listening in silence, seeking in faith and love the hidden Bridegroom, we adapt ourselves to the mode of the incomprehensible God's self-communication. For though transcendent, God has stooped down to us and spoken that loving Word, the Word who will lift us beyond ourselves into the mystery. John insists on our adapting ourselves in contemplation to God's mode of giving.

Since God, then, as the giver communes with individuals through a simple, loving knowledge, they also, as the receivers, commune with God through a simple and loving knowledge or attention, so that knowledge is thus joined with knowledge and love with love. The receiver should act according to the mode of what is received, and not otherwise, in order to receive and keep it in the way it is given. For as the philosophers say: Whatever is received is received according to the mode of the receiver.

. . . If souls should, then, desire to act on their own through an attitude different from the passive loving attention we mentioned, in which they would remain very passive and tranquil without making any act, unless God would unite himself with them in some act, they would utterly hinder the goods God communicates supernaturally to them in the loving knowledge. This loving knowledge is communicated in the beginning through the exercise of interior purgation, in which the individual suffers, as we said, and afterward in the delight of love.

If as I say—and it is true—this loving knowledge is received passively in the soul according to the supernatural mode of God, and not according to the natural mode of the soul, individuals, if they want to receive it, should be very annihilated in their natural operations, unhampered, idle, quiet, peaceful, and serene, according to the mode of God. The more the air is cleansed of vapors, and the quieter and more simple it is, the more the sun illumines and warms it. A person should not bear attachment to anything, neither to the practice of meditation, nor to any savor, whether sensory or spiritual, nor to any other apprehensions. Individuals should be very free and annihilated regarding all things, because any thought or discursive reflection or satisfaction on which they may want to lean would impede and disquiet them and make noise in the profound silence of their senses and their spirit, which they possess for the sake of this deep and delicate listening. God speaks to the heart in this solitude, which he mentioned in Hosea [Hos. 2:14], in supreme peace and tranquillity; while the soul listens, like David, to what the Lord God speaks to it [Ps. 85:8], for he speaks this peace in this solitude. (F 3.34)

Here John equates the term "supernatural" with passivity. The Holy Spirit is divinizing the soul according to the divine mode of acting. The contemplative merely receives quietly and simply what God is giving. The quiet is bred out of the detachment engendered through the theological life. John, then, has this advice for spiritual guides:

When a soul approaches this state, strive that it become detached from all satisfaction, relish, pleasure, and spiritual meditations, and do not disquiet it with cares and solicitude about heavenly things or, still less, earthly things. Bring it to as complete a withdrawal and solitude as possible, for the more solitude it obtains and the nearer it approaches this idle tranquillity the more abundantly will the spirit of divine wisdom be infused into its soul. This wisdom is loving, tranquil, solitary, peaceful, mild, and an inebriator of the spirit, by which the soul feels tenderly and gently wounded and carried away, without knowing by whom or from where or how. The reason is that this wisdom is communicated without the soul's own activity. (F 3.38)

Sometimes God, this boundless desert who remains always beyond our complete reach, becomes spiritually more perceptible while the contemplative remains in passive stillness.

Not for this reason alone do we call mystical wisdom "secret" —and it is actually so—but also because it has the characteristic of hiding the soul within itself. Besides its usual effect, this mystical wisdom will occasionally so engulf souls in its secret abyss that they will have the keen awareness of being brought into a place far removed from every creature. They will accordingly feel that they have been led into a remarkably deep and vast wilderness, unattainable by any human creature, into an immense, unbounded desert, the more delightful, savorous, and loving, the deeper, vaster, and more solitary it is. They are conscious of being so much more hidden the more they are elevated above every temporal creature.

Souls are so elevated and exalted by this abyss of wisdom, which leads them into the veins of the science of love, that they realize that all the conditions of creatures in relation to this supreme knowing and divine experience are very base, and they perceive the lowliness, deficiency, and inadequacy of all the terms and words used in this life to deal with divine things. They will also note the impossibility, without the illumination of this mystical theology, of a knowledge or experience of these divine things, as they are in themselves, through any natural means, no matter how wisely or loftily one speaks of them. Beholding this truth—that it can neither grasp nor explain this wisdom—the soul rightly calls it secret. (N 2.17.4–6)

This moving description of pure contemplation (mystical theology), in which the transcendent God is keenly experienced and tasted, helps us understand why John insists that we seek God as hidden, in the general, loving attention of faith and love. Although contemplation consists of both knowledge and love, the knowledge, which is always a knowledge bestowed according to the mode of faith, is not clear. This allows for an experience seemingly dissimilar to our ordinary experience, in which the appetite follows upon perception, or love follows knowledge.

"Or," you will say, "when the intellect does not understand particular things, the will is idle and does not love (something that must always be avoided on the spiritual road), because the will can only love what the intellect understands." This is true, especially in the natural operations and acts of the soul, in which the will does not love except what the intellect understands distinctly. But in the contemplation we are discussing (by which God infuses himself into the soul), particular knowledge as well as acts made by the soul are unnecessary. The reason for this is that God in one act is communicating light and love together, which is loving supernatural knowledge. We can assert that this knowledge is like light that transmits heat, for that light also enkindles love. This knowledge is general and dark to the intellect because it is contemplative knowledge, which is a ray of darkness for the intellect, as St. Dionysius teaches.

Love is therefore present in the will in the manner that knowledge is present in the intellect. Just as this knowledge infused by God in the intellect is general and dark, devoid of particular understanding, the love in the will is also general, without any clarity arising from particular understanding. Since God is divine light and love in his communication of himself to the soul, he equally informs these two faculties (intellect and will) with knowledge and love. Since God is unintelligible in this life, knowledge of him is dark, as I say, and the love present in the will is fashioned after this knowledge.

Yet sometimes in this delicate communication, God wounds and communicates himself to one faculty more than to the other; sometimes more knowledge is experienced than love, and at other times more love than knowledge; and likewise at times all knowledge is felt without any love, or all love without any knowledge.

This is why I say that when the soul makes natural acts with the intellect, it cannot love without understanding. But in the acts God produces and infuses in it, as he does in these souls, there is a difference; God can communicate to one faculty and not to the other. He can inflame the will with a touch of the warmth of his love even though the intellect does not understand, just as a person can feel warmth from a fire without seeing it.

The will often feels enkindled or tenderly moved or captivated without knowing how or understanding anything more particularly than before, since God is ordaining love in it; as the bride declares in the Song of Songs: "The king brought me into the wine cellar and set in order charity in me" [Song 2:4]. (F 3.49–50)

## The Weight of God's Gentle Hand

Although the soul may be tenderly captivated without knowing how in the darkness of God's transcendence, this divine wisdom can also at times turn into an affliction and a torment. The two reasons for this lie in the height of the divine wisdom intensifying the feeling of darkness, and a sharper awareness of one's own baseness and unholiness. Yet John interprets this as God merely attempting to draw near.

How amazing and pitiful it is that the soul be so utterly weak and impure that the hand of God, though light and gentle, should feel so heavy and contrary. For the hand of God does not press down or weigh on the soul, but only touches it; and this mercifully, for God's aim is to grant it favors and not chastise it. (N 2.5.7)

This is what John calls the passive night of the spirit, an experience of purgative contemplation described so vividly by him that he has frightened many of his readers. But what is happening should be cherished like the dawn of day since the transcendent God is seeking to draw close to us human beings and disclose and share the divine life in intimacy with us. The root of the piercing pain lies in the lack of holiness on the part of humans, not in the contemplation, which only brings to the fore what did not previously lay in plain view—deep-rooted things. God has not willed to be solely the transcendent. In the mystery of Jesus he has reached down and become also our immanent God wanting to raise us up. In the process of being raised up, we undergo paradoxically the feeling of being cast down.

Another excellence of dark contemplation, its majesty and grandeur ... makes the soul feel within itself the other extreme—its own intimate poverty and misery. Such awareness is one of the chief afflictions it suffers in the purgation.

The soul experiences an emptiness and poverty in regard to three classes of goods (temporal, natural, and spiritual) which are directed toward pleasing it, and is conscious of being placed in the midst of the contrary evils (the miseries of imperfections, aridities and voids in the apprehensions of the faculties, and an abandonment of the spirit in darkness). (N 2.6.4)

This contemplation produces the very results that should be the aim of any personal struggle to grow close to God through the theological life. Faith, hope, and love are increasingly gaining predominance in the journey, but now through pain as they bring about the final sigh of the old self. In explaining this dark night John limits himself to explain what God through the divine self-communication is doing when one feels such poverty and misery. Purgative contemplation, however, does not exist in isolation from the rest of life; it comes generally tethered to stormy, life situations, all a part of divine providence. John of the Cross himself, slowly wasting away in the tomb-like prison cell of Toledo, with no physical or human comfort, suffered a dark night that was more than inward. Human beings suffer dark nights in many ways, particularly in their relationships with others. There may be disloyalty and damaged reputations. Sharp thorns of persecution can pierce the heart after efforts to stay faithful to God's will. Children or elderly parents sometimes cry out for a tender care that drains all human capacity. Young adults may break a parent's heart. Unexpected failure in ministry or career might betray all life's dreams. One may have to cope with persons whose discordant personalities disrupt the peaceful functioning of a community. Poverty, discrimination, oppression can make life resemble the bottom of a pit. All of these and many other tragedies and pains that plague a human life can be fiber for the fabric of the dark night. But suffering in itself does not purify or constitute the dark night of which John of the Cross speaks. In his sense, the dark night essentially comprises the theological life, of which contemplation is a part, the desire to push forward in pursuit of the Beloved alone—though one's face may be metaphorically prostrate in the dust—in complete trust that the Beloved will not abandon anyone who seeks him. In reality God is actually reaching down to his bride that she might stretch up to him.

As a result the soul must first be set in emptiness and poverty of spirit and purged of every natural support, consolation, and apprehension, earthly and heavenly. Thus empty, it is truly poor in spirit and stripped of the old self, and thereby able to live that new and blessed life which is the state of union with God, attained by means of this night. (N 2.9.9)

Once the soul is emptied of everything, it feels a vast void, for any little thing can so hold our attention and absorb us that we do not perceive what we lack.

It is an amazing thing that the least of these goods is enough so to encumber these faculties, capable of infinite goods, that they cannot receive these infinite goods until they are completely empty, as we shall see. Yet when these caverns are empty and pure, the thirst, hunger, and yearning of the spiritual feeling is intolerable. Since these caverns have deep stomachs, they suffer profoundly; for the food they lack, which as I say is God, is also profound. (F 3.18)

### Impassioned Love

Spiritual darkness and hunger create the climate for the touches and wounds of love that increase the soul's thirst. The wound of love may be delightful or painful. It is painful when the Beloved is felt to be absent at the same time that the love and longing are being intensified. In this thirst of love, the observance of the first commandment, the norm for the use of all one's abilities, becomes the principal care of one's life.

One might, then, in a certain way ponder how remarkable and how strong this enkindling of love in the spirit can be. God gathers together all the strength, faculties, and appetites of the soul, spiritual and sensory alike, that the energy and power of this whole harmonious composite may be employed in this love. The soul consequently arrives at the true fulfillment of the first com-

mandment which, neither disdaining anything human nor exclud-
ing it from this love, states: "You shall love your God with your
whole heart, and with your whole mind, and with your whole
soul, and with all your strength" [Deut. 6:5]. (N 2.11.4)

But should it happen that the enkindling and thirst and wound
of love not be felt, the love does not thereby cease to be. The love
then expresses itself in the anguish of thinking that God has been
lost. Persons of this kind esteem God so highly that they will
leave nothing undone and would long to go to the ends of the
earth if they could thereby serve and please God more.

John of the Cross also speaks of this love here as an impassioned love. We need to keep in mind that whenever he speaks of
the wounds and touches of love, or impassioned love, or the
enkindling of love, he is speaking of the emotions or affections of
love. These in themselves are not free acts of the will, since an act
of the will is such only insofar as it is free. Strictly speaking, the
enkindling of love and the wound of love are not love in itself,
because they do not proceed from a free act of the will. Worth
mentioning as well is the fact that through such terminology
John is actually speaking of the subject as doer, as one who delib-
erates, evaluates, chooses, and acts. By her own acts the bride
makes herself what she is to be, and she does so freely and
responsibly. Indeed, her acts are the free and responsible expressions of herself.

The enkindling is felt in the spiritual substance of the soul. The
substance in this context is the capacity the spirit possesses for
feeling fruition, delight, and joy; or anguish, sadness, and deso-
lation. The enkindling may take place in the sensory substance,
as is the case in the fervent feelings and consolations of beginners
or in the spiritual substance as happens in contemplation.

John points out further that the inflaming of love is felt at first
more than the contemplative understanding and explains the
reason why.

We may answer that this passive love does not act upon the
will directly because the will is free, and that this burning love
is more the passion of love than a free act of the will. The

warmth of love wounds the substance of the soul and thus moves the affections passively. As a result the enkindling of love is called the passion of love rather than a free act of the will. An act of the will is such only insofar as it is free. Yet, since these passions and affections bear a relation to the will, it is said that if the soul is impassioned with some affection, the will is. This is true, because the will thus becomes captive and loses its freedom, carried away by the impetus and force of the passion. As a result we say that this enkindling of love takes place in the will, that is, the appetites of the will are enkindled. This enkindling is called the passion of love rather than the free exercise of the will. (N 2.13.3)

As for the cognitive aspect of contemplation, God's communication can at times influence this dimension more than the appetitive part. The effects of these various ways in which contemplation is bestowed are discernible.

Since this dark night of contemplation consists of divine light and love—just as fire gives off both light and heat—it is not incongruous that this loving light, when communicated, sometimes acts more upon the will through the fire of love. Then the intellect is left in darkness, not being wounded by the light. At other times, this loving light illumines the intellect with understanding and leaves the will in dryness. All of this is similar to feeling the warmth of fire without seeing its light or seeing the light without feeling the fire's heat. The Lord works in this way because he infuses contemplation as he wills. (N 2.12.7)

Into that night of misery, poverty, dryness, darkness, thirst, and wounds of love, Christ the Bridegroom will enter and, moved by compassion, reveal his loving presence. The dark night is not a matter of measuring up to a standard but of an encounter between lovers—one divine, the other mortal and weak.

It should be known that the loving Bridegroom of souls cannot long watch them suffering alone—as this soul is suffering—because as he says through Zechariah, their afflictions touch

him in the apple of his eye [Zech. 2:8]; especially when these
afflictions are the outcome of love for him, as are those of this
soul. . . .

Apparently God granted a certain spiritual feeling of his presence to this loving soul whose prayers are so enkindled. . . .
He revealed some deep glimpses of his divinity and beauty by
which he greatly increased her fervor and desire to see him.
As a man throws water into the forge to stir up and intensify
the fire, so the Lord usually grants to some souls that walk in
these fiery longings of love certain signs of his excellence to
make them more fervent and further prepare them for the
favors he wishes to grant them later. (C 11.1)

A glance at what is beautiful suffices to give birth to *erōs*,
which is an élan, a force that drives us unrelentingly toward the
beautiful, a desire to possess it. Plato is noted for his exposition
in the *Symposium* of a dialectical ascent that carries the lover from
the love of beautiful bodies to the love of beautiful spirits, and
then from the love of beautiful spirits to the love of Beauty in
itself and through itself. Next to this beauty, no other beauty any
longer has value, especially corporeal beauty.

In John's *Spiritual Canticle*, created beauty is like a trace of the
beauty of Christ and increases the bride's desire to see him. In
contemplation the Bridegroom sometimes visits her and gives
her glimpses of his divine beauty that intensely increase her
longing to possess him. In these visits she experiences for some
moments his loving presence and communication.

Yet insofar as this soul is full of fervor and tender love of God,
we should understand that this presence she asks the Beloved
to reveal refers chiefly to a certain affective presence that the
Beloved accords her. This presence is so sublime that the soul
feels that an immense hidden being is there from which God
communicates to her some semi-clear glimpses of his divine
beauty. And these bear such an effect on the soul that she
ardently longs and faints with desire for what she feels hidden
there in that presence. (C 11.4)

Since no other human person will ever satisfy the drive of eros completely, people fall in and out of love. The Greek terms *erōs* and *agapē* need not be set in opposition, nor should *erōs* be lumped together with sexual desire, which can occur without *erōs*. Christian charity, if allowed, will transform all human forms of love. These human forms include affection, friendship, and *erōs*. What John makes clear but might come as a surprise to us in regard to *erōs*, is that Christian love does not leave it buried in a tomb.

Considering the movement of transcendence from the perspectives of Christian revelation and the experience of Christian saints, we find that it is Christ ultimately who satisfies the drive of *erōs* in us. Although *erōs* is usually experienced in relation to a human lover, it is in reality a heavenly force. In John's valid view of Christian belief, the infinitely transcendent God chooses to create so as to go out in love to a bride.

Christ on the cross reminds all those who seek union with God how *erōs* must undergo a crucifixion: "Those who are of Christ have crucified their flesh with its passions and its desires" (Gal. 5:24).

The journey, then, does not consist in consolations, delights, and spiritual feelings, but in the living death of the cross, sensory and spiritual, exterior and interior. (A 2.7.11)

Struggling toward crucifixion of all the corrupted activities of the old self, we receive the strong grace to imitate the crucifixion of the one whose love is incorruptible. Yet the crucifixion of *erōs* does not kill *erōs*, doesn't even dispel it, but awakens and transforms it. In the bare sepulcher of the dark night, the hollowing hunger for the Beloved Christ increases, and there is moaning for a visit from the Beloved. In all contemplation, the bride is variously drawn out of herself in a desire to be completely possessed by the beloved Bridegroom, and pressed to give herself completely to him. The principal care is not so much transcending self, but the gift of self.

# Chapter 11

# On the Mountaintop

Envisioning the spiritual journey as a climb to the top of a mountain, John of the Cross, presenting the summit as goal of the journey, calls that goal "union of a soul with God." Although he also refers to it as the "high state of perfection," he prefers the word "union," which he uses in various combined forms: the union of love, the union through love, the divine union, the perfect union of the soul with God, the state of perfect union. Sometimes he just uses the name "God." The soul ascends to God.

"Transformation" is another expression he frequently uses for the same reality: transformation of the soul in God, divine transformation, the transformation of the soul in God through love, or the transformation of love. But he never uses the popular, less precise expression "transforming union."

There is a union with God that always exists by means of which God sustains us as the ground of our being and without which we would crumble into nothingness. This is not the union John is speaking of when focusing on the summit of the "Mount of Perfection." The union he perceives as the aim of the spiritual journey is, as he calls it, "the union of the likeness of love." This union comes about through God's grace, when a person casts off everything unconformed to the divine will. John uses three metaphors to suggest something of the reality of this union, one of which we have already seen: the light illuminating the window; the action of fire on a log of wood; and marriage between bride and groom.

### The Illumined Window

Here is an example that will provide a better understanding of this explanation. A ray of sunlight shining on a smudgy window is unable to illumine that window completely and transform it into its own light. It could do this if the window were cleaned and polished. The less the film and stain are wiped away, the less the window will be illumined; and the cleaner the window is, the brighter will be its illumination. . . . Although obviously the nature of the window is distinct from that of the sun's ray (even if the two seem identical), we can assert that the window is the ray or light of the sun by participation. The soul on which the divine light of God's being is ever shining, or better, in which it is ever dwelling by nature, is like this window, as we have affirmed. . . .

When God grants this supernatural favor to the soul, so great a union is caused that all the things of both God and the soul become one in participant transformation, and the soul appears to be God more than a soul. Indeed, it is God by participation. Yet truly, its being (even though transformed) is naturally as distinct from God's as it was before, just as the window, although illumined by the ray, has being distinct from the ray's. (A 2.5.6–7)

What makes a soul like God? A new form. The word "transformation," by reason of its prefix, denotes a change or mutation with respect to the form. In the word "conform" or "conformity" the prefix denotes the concurrence or company of persons or things. To conform is to bring one thing into harmony with another. Where there is a likeness between two persons, conformity results: the two are of one accord, one will. Both "conformity" and "transformation" are derivatives of the word "form." In transformation a change of form takes place, and since John speaks of the transformation of the soul in God, the soul changes its form, leaves it aside, and acquires the form of God. The passage just quoted makes it clear that John is not dealing with a change of substance in the strictly ontological sense; the divine Being would still be infinitely distinct from the soul.

The new form is the theological life, God's self-communication that brings about a change in us. The word "transformation" can refer to the action of transforming or to the work realized through this action. Conformity follows when the work of transformation is effected. The two things or persons are in accord, in agreement; they are alike with respect to the form. Both transformation (when effected) and conformity signify likeness. For John of the Cross, then, when two things or persons are conformed or alike you have a union, but a specific kind of union: a union of likeness or conformity (transformation effected). The meaning of these terms, though clear enough in John's time, may be too quickly presumed in our own, especially when comparing with one another the mystical teachings found in different religions.

### The Log in the Fire

The next image used by John illustrates these ideas further, expressing more vividly the work of purification that necessarily precedes the union:

The soul is purged and prepared for union with the divine light just as the wood is prepared for transformation into the fire. Fire, when applied to wood, first dehumidifies it, dispelling all moisture and making it give off any water it contains. Then it gradually turns the wood black, makes it dark and ugly, and even causes it to emit a bad odor. By drying out the wood, the fire brings to light and expels all those ugly and dark accidents that are contrary to fire. Finally, by heating and enkindling it from without, the fire transforms the wood into itself and makes it as beautiful as it is itself. Once transformed the wood no longer has any activity or passivity of its own, except for its weight and its quantity which is denser than the fire. For it possesses the properties and performs the actions of fire: it is dry and it dries; it is hot and it gives off heat; it is brilliant and it illumines; it is also much lighter in weight than before. It is the fire that produces all these properties in the wood. (N 2.10.1)

This engaging image is a fine illustration of how the work of purification is actually a work of divinization. Once a person has reached union, the divinization is realized and that person lives a divinized or divine life. Here is another passage from the *Dark Night* that sums up the theory behind the image:

These proficients are still very lowly and natural in their communion with God and in their activity directed toward him because the gold of the spirit is not purified and illumined. They still think of God and speak of him as little children, and their knowledge and experience of him is like that of little children, as St. Paul asserts [1 Cor. 13:11]. The reason is that they have not reached perfection, which is union of the soul with God. Through this union, as fully grown, they do mighty works in their spirit since their faculties and works are more divine than human, as we will point out. Wishing to strip them in fact of this old self and clothe them with the new, which is created according to God in the newness of sense, as the Apostle says [Col. 3:9–10; Eph. 4:22–24; Rom. 12:2], God divests the faculties, affections, and senses, both spiritual and sensory, interior and exterior. He leaves the intellect in darkness, the will in aridity, the memory in emptiness, and the affections in supreme affliction, bitterness, and anguish by depriving the soul of the feeling and satisfaction it previously obtained from spiritual blessings. For this privation is one of the conditions required that the spiritual form, which is the union of love, may be introduced into the spirit and united with it. (N 2.3.3)

The life of the old self, of the old form, is death because it is an impediment to the "perfect" spiritual life, which is the true life, the new form. Centering her activity on God (the knowledge, love, and service of God), the soul will live the divine, resplendent life of the new self. At the root of all genuine purification is the expulsion (putting to death) of the inordinate affections for creatures through the forceful love of God, which is the root and substance of the entire transformation of the soul in God. The following long passage from the *Living Flame of Love* dwells on this

process of dying in order to have life and supports the teaching
with texts from Scripture, particularly St. Paul:

For death is nothing else than the privation of life, because
when life comes no vestige of death remains. Spiritually speaking, there are two kinds of life:

One is beatific, consisting in the vision of God, which must
be attained by natural death, as St. Paul says: "We know that
if this our clay house is dissolved, we have a dwelling place of
God in heaven" [2 Cor. 5:1].

The other is the perfect spiritual life, the possession of God
through union of love. This is acquired through complete mortification of all the vices and appetites and of one's own nature.
Until this is achieved, one cannot reach the perfection of the
spiritual life of union with God; as the Apostle also declares in
these words: "If you live according to the flesh you shall die;
yet if with the spirit you mortify the deeds of the flesh you
shall live" [Rom. 8:13].

Let it be known that what the soul calls death is all that
goes to make up the old self: the entire engagement of the
faculties (memory, intellect, and will) in the things of the world,
and the indulgence of the appetites in the pleasures of creatures. All this is the activity of the old life, which is the death
of the new spiritual life. The soul is unable to live perfectly in
this new life, if the old self does not die completely. The Apostle
warns: "Take off the old self and put on the new self who
according to God is created in justice and holiness" [Eph. 4:22–
24]. In this new life that the soul lives when it has arrived at
the perfect union with God here being discussed, all the inclinations and activity of the appetites and faculties, which of its
own was the operation of death and the privation of the spiritual life, become divine.

Since every living being lives by its operations, as the philosophers say, and the soul's operations are in God through its
union with him, it lives the life of God. Thus it changed its
death to life, its animal life to spiritual life.

The intellect, which before this union understood naturally
by the vigor of its natural light, by means of the natural senses,

is now moved and informed by another higher principle of supernatural divine light, and the senses are bypassed. Accordingly, the intellect becomes divine, because through its union with God's intellect both become one.

And the will, which previously loved in a base and deadly way, only with its natural affection, is now changed into the life of divine love, for it loves in a lofty way, with divine affection, moved by the strength of the Holy Spirit in which it now lives the life of love. By means of this union, God's will and the soul's will are now one.

And the memory, which by itself perceived only the figures and phantasms of creatures, is changed through this union so as to have in its mind the eternal years mentioned by David [Ps. 77:5].

And the natural appetite, which only had the ability and strength to relish creatures (which causes death), is changed now so that its taste and savor are divine, and it is moved and satisfied by another principle: the delight of God, in which it is more alive. And because it is united with him, it is no longer anything else than the appetite of God.

Finally all the movements, operations, and inclinations the soul had previously from the principle and strength of its natural life are now in this union dead to what they formerly were, changed into divine movements, and alive to God. For the soul, like a true daughter of God, is moved in all by the Spirit of God, as St. Paul teaches in saying that those who are moved by the Spirit of God are children of God himself [Rom. 8:14].

Accordingly, the intellect of this soul is God's intellect; its will is God's will; its memory is the memory of God; and its delight is God's delight; and although the substance of this soul is not the substance of God, since it cannot undergo a substantial conversion into him, it has become God through participation in God, being united to and absorbed in him, as it is in this state. Such a union is wrought in this perfect state of the spiritual life, yet not as perfectly as in the next life. Consequently the soul is dead to all that it was in itself, which was death to it, and alive to what God is in himself. Speaking of itself, the soul declares in this verse: "In killing you changed death to life."

The soul can well repeat the words of St. Paul: "I live, now not I, but Christ lives in me" [Gal. 2:20]. The death of this soul is changed to the life of God. We can also apply the words of the Apostle *absorpta est mors in victoria* [1 Cor. 15:54], as well as those the prophet Hosea speaks in the person of God: "O death, I will be your death" [Hos. 13:14]. In other words: Since I am life, being the death of death, death will be absorbed in life. (F 2.32–34)

### The Flaring of the Flame

Within this state of divinization in which a person lives habitually the divinized life, in conformity with God's will, in the union of love, there come brimming moments in which God's self-communication is bestowed with greater intensity. John calls these ardent experiences of union "actual, transitory unions" because they come and go without rule and may be frequent or infrequent. The experiences he describes in his *Spiritual Canticle* and in the *Living Flame of Love* belong largely in this category. It is important for a reader while reading these commentaries to be alert as to when John is speaking of a passing experience rather than the ordinary, more subdued, habitual state.

We can compare the soul in its ordinary condition in this state of transformation of love to the log of wood that is ever immersed in fire, and the acts of this soul to the flame that blazes up from the fire of love. The more intense the fire of union, the more vehemently does this fire burst into flames. The acts of the will are united to this flame and ascend, carried away and absorbed in the flame of the Holy Spirit, just as the angel mounted to God in the flame of Manoah's sacrifice [Judg. 13:20]. (F 1.4)

These moments of intense absorption of the faculties in the

*rind*

knowledge and love of God as well as the different effects produced by them (for example, the inclination toward various
kinds of good works) are also imaged by John in numerous ways.
He speaks of living flames, awakenings, illuminations, lights,
visits from God or from the Bridegroom, favors, gifts, messages,
wounds of love, knowledge, anointings, unctions, touches, and
communications. Clearly, these many images suggest the multiplicity of experiences that can be effected in the spirit by the
loving knowledge of God. The two latter images (touches and
communications), used in a more general sense, include all the
others.

God touches the soul by means of the senses when communicating the "spiritual substance" by means of forms, figures, or
sensible images, which are the rind, the accident, or the vesture,
of the spiritual substance. God touches the soul without the
means of the senses when communicating the spiritual substance
(the loving knowledge) without sensible forms, that is, without
the rind, accident, or vesture. John calls this the "touch of pure
substance," the "touch of the naked substance," "the substantial
touch," "essential communication."

We communicate when we transmit information, as in conversing with another. Though we call this activity "communication," we can also by the term refer to that which is being
communicated. A communication of intimate friendship will
include endearing conversation as well as the thoughts and affections manifested or made known in this sharing, together with
the enjoyment or fruition that comes as a consequence. The terms
"communication" and "touches" in John's writings have the
same broad extension, including under their umbrella meditations as well as visions and contemplation.

Concerning the actual union, as against the habitual union,
John insists on the diversity of ways in which God deals with us,
wishing to prevent us from concluding that what he describes is
what others uniformly experience. He sets down his consequen-
tial rule at an appropriate moment in his *Spiritual Canticle:*

Yet it must not be thought that [God] communicates to all

those who reach this state everything declared in these two stanzas, or that he does so in the same manner and measure of knowledge and feeling. To some souls he gives more and to others less, to some in one way and to others in another, although all alike may be in this same state of spiritual betrothal. But the greatest possible communication is recorded here because it includes everything else. (C 14; 15.2)

Now for a poignant description of one moment of actual union as described by John that provides a good example of his mode of speaking in this regard.

To understand this better it should be noted that just as two things are felt in the breeze (the touch and the whistling or sound), so in this communication of the Bridegroom two things are experienced: knowledge and a feeling of delight. As the feeling of the breeze delights the sense of touch, and its whistling the sense of hearing, so the feeling of the Beloved's attributes are felt and enjoyed by the soul's power of touch, which is in its substance, and the knowledge of these attributes is experienced in its hearing, which is the intellect.

It should also be known that the love-stirring breeze is said to come when it wounds in a pleasant way by satisfying the appetite of the one desiring such refreshment, for the sense of touch is then filled with enjoyment and refreshment; and the hearing, at the moment of this delectable touch, experiences great pleasure and gratification in the sound and whistling of the breeze....

Since this touch of God gives intense satisfaction and enjoyment to the substance of the soul, and gently fulfills her desire for this union, she calls this union or these touches "love-stirring breezes." As we have said, the Beloved's attributes are lovingly and sweetly communicated in this breeze, and from it the intellect receives the knowledge or whistling.

She calls the knowledge a "whistling" because just as the whistling of the breeze pierces deeply into the hearing organ, so this most subtle and delicate knowledge penetrates with wonderful savoriness into the innermost part of the substance of the soul, and the delight is greater than all others.

The reason for the delight is that the substance, understood and stripped of accidents and phantasms, is bestowed. For this knowledge is given to that intellect that philosophers call the passive or possible intellect, and the intellect receives it passively without any effort of its own. . . .

This divine whistling, which enters through the soul's hearing, is not only, as I have said, the substance understood, but also an unveiling of truths about the divinity and a revelation of God's secrets. . . .

It must not be thought that, because what the soul understands is the naked substance, there is perfect and clear fruition as in heaven. Although the knowledge is stripped of accidents, it is not for this reason clear, but dark, for it is contemplation, which in this life, as St. Dionysius says, is a ray of darkness. (C 14; 15.13–16)

In pondering a text like this, we could easily conclude that God reserves favors like these for those who have served in countless remarkable ways, but John's conclusion is different. A spiritual director will never be able to understand why God would give graces like these to one person and not another.

These favors are not dependent on the works or reflections of the soul, though these exercises do dispose it well for the reception of such gifts. For God grants them to whom he wills and for the reason he wills. It can happen that someone will have done many works, and yet God will not bestow these touches; and another will have accomplished far fewer works and nevertheless receive an abundance of the most sublime touches. Accordingly, although it may be a better preparation, it is unnecessary for a person to be actually employed and occupied in spiritual matters in order that God grant the touches from which it experiences these feelings. Most of the time this favor is given when it is farthest from the mind (A 2.32.2)

## Bride and Bridegroom

The images of the window illumined by light and the wood acted
on by fire clarify the dynamic process of purification and the
need for it if there is going to be such a likeness that the window
will glisten like the light and the wood glow like the fire. Yet
these images speak of things, while the union is between persons, between devoted lover and beloved. In this love between
persons the affection of each is drawn out to the other to wish
and do good for the loved one. Where there is friendship, the
goal of the action of love is precisely the good of the other. Where
such love of friendship is not present, people seek in others
something good for themselves. True friendship is reciprocal,
moving lover and beloved to cherish and help each other. But
each is able thereby to go out of self into the will and life of the
other so that a common good comes into being at some level.
Before only the good of the self stood in one's view and blocked
all the fruition that follows when love is directed to the good of
the other.

Love disposes the senses and intellect to dwell on the beloved
to the point of setting aside everything else. It ordains the lover's
will to the good of the beloved for the beloved's sake, so that the
lover's affection is rightly said to pass out of itself in care and
provision for the beloved. When the affection is wholly imbued
by the form of the good that is its object, it takes delight in that
object and adheres to it as though fixed on it. In this way love is
nothing but a certain transformation of affection into the beloved;
through love the one loving becomes one with the beloved
because the latter is made the form of the one loving.

The ultimate of love is the unconditional surrender of one's
intellect and will to another. Only God deserves such total surrender. In what John calls "the spiritual marriage," the soul surrenders the entire possession of self to God. Thus, marriage,
celebrated in the poetry of the Song of Songs and carried over as
an image into the church's liturgy and tradition, is an exceptionally powerful symbol for conveying the intense fervor of the
mutual personal love that can exist between a soul and God.

In the *Spiritual Canticle* John of the Cross recounts, not without mystery, the story of his love for Christ, a love in response to Christ's love for him. Essentially dynamic, the love presses forward, marking degrees or stages of John's spiritual life, which develops along lines parallel with and dependent on love. The poem tells this story in the form of an eclogue, a love story between shepherdess and shepherd, bride and bridegroom. Among his works, this was, it seems, John's favorite. It speaks with passion of God's love for John and John's love for God. The mystery contained in this work and suggested by it could be summed up in two words: love and beauty. The poetic symbols delineate an increasingly intimate communion with the divine Bridegroom by means of an increasingly elevated knowledge and love of his coming through favors, visits, wounds, and touches of love.

The hunger and thirst for union with the Beloved Christ increase to the point that the bride is able to go out of herself completely in a total gift of self to the Beloved.

God causes in this union the purity and perfection necessary for such a surrender. And since he transforms her in himself, he makes her entirely his own and empties her of all she possesses other than him.

Hence, not only in her will but also in her works she is really and totally given to God, without keeping anything back, just as God has freely given himself entirely to her. This union is so effected that the two wills are mutually paid, surrendered, and satisfied (so that neither fails the other in anything) with the fidelity and stability of an espousal. She therefore adds:

There I promised to be his bride.

Just as one who is espoused does not love, care, or work for any other than her bridegroom, so the soul in this state has no affections of the will or knowledge in the intellect or care or work or appetite that is not entirely inclined toward God. She is as it were divine and deified, in such a way that in regard to all she can understand she does not even suffer the first movements contrary to God's will.

As an imperfect soul is ordinarily inclined toward evil, at least in the first movements of its will, intellect, memory, and appetites, and as it has imperfections, so on the other hand the soul in this state ordinarily inclines and moves toward God in the first movements of its intellect, memory, will, and appetites, because of the great help and stability it has in God and its perfect conversion toward him.

David clarified all this when he said, speaking of the soul in this state: "Shall not my soul be subject to God? Yes; for from him do I receive salvation, and because he is my God and my Savior and my rock I shall no longer move" [Ps. 62:1-2]. By using the expression, my rock, he indicates that since his soul is set firmly in God and united to him, it will no longer suffer any movement contrary to God.... She is conscious that love is so valuable in her Beloved's sight that he neither esteems nor makes use of anything else but love, and so she employs all her strength in the pure love of God, desiring to serve him perfectly.

She does this not merely because he desires it, but also because the love by which she is united to him moves her to the love of God in and through all things. Like the bee that sucks honey from all the wildflowers and will not use them for anything else, the soul easily extracts the sweetness of love from all the things that happen to her; that is, she loves God in them. Thus everything leads her to love. And being informed and fortified as she is with love, she neither feels nor tastes nor knows the things that happen to her, whether delightful or bitter, since as we said the soul knows nothing else but love. And her pleasure in all things and in all transactions is always the delight of loving God. (C 27.6-8)

# Chapter 12

# "That They May Be One in Us"

Some people are not at ease thinking of God as friend, companion, or beloved. They prefer to conceive of God as mystery surrounding human life, to live in the hush of darkness. They choose to be apophatic before God, to remain silent in the presence of the ultimately unspeakable mystery. In much of the *Ascent of Mount Carmel*, John of the Cross underscores God's transcendence and incomprehensibility, and the paltry nature of our understanding of the divine mystery.

There are people, however, who complain that the *Ascent* is too negative, finding themselves much more comfortably at home with the *Spiritual Canticle*, where emphasis is laid on friendship, love, and personal relationship. Certainly, no progress can be made in the spiritual life without love, and love is between persons. However, the love between God and a soul should not be confused with sentimentality. Love, as everyone knows, need not always be experienced as emotion.

But a person does not always grasp or feel this love, because it does not reside with tenderness in the senses, but resides in the soul with properties of strength and of greater courage and daring than before. (A 2.24.9)

Although the mystery of God's transcendence may stand out more prominently for some, and the mystery of his immanence for others, it would be a wonder if the spiritual life of a Christian were to exclude either entirely. Both experiences have their times and seasons. For one thing, we can look at the dark nights as periods in which God is experienced as absent or transcendent.

Transcendence, strictly speaking though, does not refer to God's remoteness or distance. God is always near, but the Beloved is hidden in boundless mystery; there ever remains infinitely more to know or feel. The end of our journey can never lie in what we understand or experience of God. We cannot foresee when the shadowy sense that God is absent or far away or unlovable will come over us, or when it will leave. An aspect of admitting to the incomprehensibility of God is the realization that we must relinquish all attempts to put limits on God, those many expectations that the Lord will do things only this way and not that.

All is meted out according to God's will and the greater or lesser amount of imperfection that must be purged from each one. In the measure of the degree of love to which God wishes to raise a soul, he humbles it with greater or lesser intensity, or for a longer or shorter period of time.

Those who have more considerable capacity and strength for suffering God purges more intensely and quickly. But those who are very weak he keeps in this night for a long time. Their purgation is less intense and their temptations abated, and he frequently refreshes their senses to keep them from backsliding. They arrive at the purity of perfection late in life. And some of them never reach it entirely, for they are never wholly in the night or wholly out of it. Although they do not advance, God exercises them for short periods and on certain days in those temptations and aridities to preserve them in humility and self-knowledge; and at other times and seasons he comes to their aid with consolation, lest through loss of courage they return to their search after worldly consolation. God acts with other weaker souls as though he were showing himself and then hiding; he does this to exercise them in his love, for without these withdrawals they would not learn to reach him. (N 1.14.5)

## The Spousal Relationship

Many saints have discovered in the Song of Songs ideal expressions of their contemplative experiences of Christ revealing his love for them. It is in the depths of dark contemplation that the soul is ultimately liberated from the world, the devil, and her own sensuality, and there that she begins to perceive and speak without strain of Christ as spouse or bridegroom. A relationship of this kind, independent of a person's sex, is not produced but given, and the imagery of the Bridegroom refers to Christ as divine. It is his radiance, like that manifested on the Mount of the Transfiguration that fuels in darkness the desire for presence and union. The kiss and the embrace take place ethereally in the spirit—a contemplative gift beyond the confines of the bodily senses and commotions. Much purification needs to take place before one is prepared to receive the intimate and exquisitely delicate communications characteristic of those between Christ and his bride.

Through her relationship with Christ the soul finds it possible to strip herself of the old life and put on the new life of the theological virtues, dispossess herself of all the concrete good things that are an obstacle to her loving and hoping in him above all things. Through his example, Christ on the cross is her sustaining force in the passage through this spiritual death.

Bear fortitude in your heart against all things that move you to that which is not God, and be a friend of the Passion of Christ. (S 95)

Because I have said that Christ is the way and that this way is a death to our natural selves in the sensory and spiritual parts of the soul, I would like to demonstrate how this death is patterned on Christ's, for he is our model and light. (A 2.7.9)

But following Christ does not end with his bare death on the cross. The human being is relational, and a person reaches fulfillment by being transformed through love into the risen Christ. It is the Holy Spirit who brings this transformation about.

### The Holy Spirit's Mission

The Holy Spirit's mission as Spirit of the Bridegroom is to prepare one for perfect union with Christ in the spiritual marriage, to transform or divinize the soul. After having discarded the old self and put on the new (Eph. 4:22–24), a person is then free and ready to be moved habitually by the Spirit.

The Holy Spirit wounds the soul by destroying and consuming the imperfections of its bad habits. . . . [the Holy Spirit] disposes it for divine union and transformation in God through love. (F 1.19)

John of the Cross develops and explains the work of the Holy Spirit with a variety of images and a rich use of biblical symbolism. Two metaphors that particularly arouse interest are the "anointing" and the "breathing."

Jesus himself received a solemn anointing at his baptism in the Jordan to mark the beginning of his messianic mission, and because of his anointing with the Holy Spirit by the Father, he is called Christ (the anointed one). Bearing the name of Christ in their title, Christians become sharers in Christ's anointing. The church is a continuation in history of the anointing of Christ with the Holy Spirit. In baptism we are anointed with chrism, which is a figure of the Holy Spirit with which Christ was anointed. In the Mass of the Chrism in Holy Week, the bishop says: "May this unction permeate them and make them holy so that, freed from the corruption of their first birth and consecrated as the temple of your glory, they may breathe forth the perfume of a holy life."

It is in treating the period between spiritual betrothal and spiritual marriage that John attends in a particular way to the anointings of the Holy Spirit as means of final preparation for the marriage to take place between the bride and Bridegroom. This would not mean that the Holy Spirit had not been preparing the soul with many anointings all along before its coming to this stage.

In point of fact, the entire work of the Spirit has as its aim an increase of the soul's desire for God, a desire for God that helps the Christian turn away from all the froth alien to the love and service of God—which includes the love and service of others, too, in right relationships. When a soul is so free of everything that she can say yes to God, then, through the yes of the soul, God gives the true and complete yes of his grace. This is called spiritual betrothal. In the spiritual marriage, on the other hand, a union between the persons takes place in such a way that each surrenders the entire possession of self to the other. It seems to the bride that she has been placed in the arms of the Bridegroom, and she experiences an intimate spiritual embrace by means of which she lives the life of God.

The visits and gifts of Christ during the time of spiritual betrothal beautify and refine the soul further to make her more suitable for the marriage. John illustrates with an instance from the book of Esther in which the maidens chosen for King Ahasuerus had to spend a year being prepared through certain precious ointments of myrrh and other spices before being brought to the king's bed. And this even though they had already been taken out of their own countries and away from their families (Esth. 2:3, 12).

The anointings of the Holy Spirit can cause extreme, impassioned longings for God in the depths of our being. These anointings of the Spirit, being more closely related to God, lure the soul and make her relish the Bridegroom more delicately so that her desires for him increase in refinement and depth. John is steadfast in his principle that the desire for God is the preparation for union with God (F 3.26). Dark purgative contemplation, then, in which the soul's anxieties and longings for the Bridegroom are heightened, is not the exclusive means of preparing one for the union of spiritual marriage. The divine visits and touches characteristic of the spiritual betrothal, which John calls anointings, also serve as a purification, effecting a final liberation of the soul.

Although it is true that this betrothal occurs in the soul that is greatly purified of every affection for creatures—for the spiritual betrothal is not wrought until this comes to pass—the soul still needs other positive preparations from God. It needs his visits and gifts by which he purifies, beautifies, and refines it further that it might be suitably prepared for so lofty a union.

This preparation takes time, for some more than for others, since God carries out this work according to the mode of the soul. (F 3.25–26)

Three objectives are being accomplished through these anointings. First, the soul is made to hunger and thirst for God as, and
in the measure that, she is filled, delighted, and satisfied by these
gifts. Second, in these refreshing visits the Holy Spirit makes the
soul acutely aware of the Bridegroom's burning desire to give
full possession of himself to her. Third, as adopted child of God,
being made completely poor in spirit, or detached from everything, the soul comes into full possession of her inheritance. St.
Paul's words are verified here: "Having nothing, yet possessing
all things" (2 Cor 6:10).

### Sharing in the Inheritance

The soul's inheritance as adopted child, John teaches, is God, the
Holy Trinity. Thus we have come to the fullness of the *nada* and
*todo*. As adopted child of God the soul shares in the birthright of
the firstborn Son, who possesses all the rich treasure of eternal
Wisdom and merits for us a participation in this patrimony. She
wants, then, to enjoy this glowing treasure of Wisdom, to look
closely at her Beloved, whom she now possesses, and know everything, all the secrets that lay in that vast solitude of his heart. The
Wisdom of that heart reaches down into so immense an abyss that
she can never reach a point where it becomes impossible to penetrate further into the incomprehensible wealth it holds. Apopha-
sis (the way of darkness, of unknowing) and kataphasis (the way
of light, of knowing)—neither can stand alone, each also requires
either some knowing or some unknowing.

One of the outstanding favors God grants briefly in this life is
an understanding and experience of himself so lucid and lofty
that one comes to know clearly that God cannot be completely
understood or experienced. This understanding is somewhat
like that of the Blessed in heaven: Those who understand God
more understand more distinctly the infinitude that remains to
be understood; those who see less of him do not realize so
clearly what remains to be seen. (C 7.9)

## Transformation into Wisdom

Divine Wisdom is not an abstract concept but a person. The divine Wisdom is the divine Word become human. When John speaks of this Wisdom as the goal of union, he does not have in mind a union with God's attribute of wisdom, but union with the only-begotten Son of God. In this he follows St. Paul, who identifies the Wisdom of the Old Testament with Jesus Christ. The soul is not called to union with a wisdom preexistent to the Word incarnate, but to union with Wisdom who is the Word, the Beloved, the Son of God, "the most sweet Jesus, Bridegroom of faithful souls."

*She*

John of the Cross identifies the material object of faith (the content of faith) with the entire mystery of Christ. Jesus Christ is not only a means to union but the ultimate object of the theological life, resplendent Wisdom in whom the soul finds All.

In giving us his Son, his only Word (for he possesses no other), [the Father] spoke everything to us at once in this sole Word —and he has no more to say.

This is the meaning of that passage where St. Paul tries to persuade the Hebrews to turn from communion with God through the old ways of the Mosaic law and instead fix their eyes on Christ: "That which God formerly spoke to our fathers through the prophets in many ways and manners, now, finally, in these days he has spoken to us all at once in his Son" [Heb. 1:1–2]. The Apostle indicates that God has become as it were mute, with no more to say, because what he spoke before to the prophets in parts, he has now spoken all at once by giving us the All, who is his Son. (A 2.22.4)

With the symbols of "mountain," "hill," and "thicket" John speaks of the soul's union, in contemplation, with the divine Wisdom, proclaiming as he does the glowing beauty of this Wisdom.

Hence the soul makes the petition that she and her Bridegroom go forth to behold each other in his beauty.

To the mountain and to the hill,

That is: to the morning and essential knowledge of God, which is knowledge in the divine Word, who in his height is signified here by the mountain. That they may know the Son of God, Isaiah urges all: "Come let us ascend to the mountain of the Lord" [Isa. 2:3]; in another passage: "The mountain of the house of the Lord shall be prepared" [Isa. 2:2].

"And to the hill," that is, to the evening knowledge of God, which is God's wisdom in his creatures, works, and wondrous decrees. The hill suggests this wisdom because it is not as high as the morning wisdom. Yet the soul asks for both the evening and the morning wisdom when she says: "To the mountain and to the hill."

The soul in urging the Bridegroom, "let us go forth to the mountain to behold ourselves in your beauty," means: Transform me into the beauty of divine Wisdom and make me resemble that which is the Word, the Son of God. And in adding "to the hill," she asks that he inform her with the beauty of this other lesser wisdom contained in his creatures and other mysterious works. This wisdom is also the beauty of the Son of God by which the soul desires to be illumined.

The soul cannot see herself in the beauty of God unless she is transformed into the wisdom of God, in which she sees herself in possession of earthly and heavenly things. . . .

To where the pure water flows,

That is, to where God bestows on the intellect knowledge and wisdom, called water here because it cleanses and removes accidents and phantasies, and clears away the clouds of ignorance. The soul always possesses this desire to have clear and pure understanding of the divine truths; and the greater her love, the more she longs to enter further into these truths. (C 36.6–9)

Being united with the uncreated Wisdom, she is united immediately with the divine Word, Son of God, eternal Wisdom, deposit of the Father's limitless treasures, figure of his sub-stance—all of which point to her insertion into the trinitarian life. Being united with created wisdom, she sees how divine provi-dence provides in time for the union of the divinity and human-ity in Jesus in the one person of the Word, how she shares in Jesus' grace flowing from his union with the being of the Word, how the divine attributes are warmly reflected there, how human beings are predestined in him, how the union of love corre-sponds to the hypostatic union, how all creation is made beauti-ful in the glory of Christ's resurrection, how the church will share the brilliant beauty of the Bridegroom in the day of her triumph.

This loving knowledge of which John speaks is not an adjunct to the full union or secondary to it. It implies a living relationship to Jesus Christ sent as teacher of the soul by the Father, for Jesus presents himself as Truth and Wisdom of the Father. But since in the end this Wisdom is incomprehensible, the mysteries of God's wisdom in Christ will never be exhausted.

However numerous are the mysteries and marvels that holy doctors have discovered and saintly souls understood in this earthly life, all the more is yet to be said and understood. There is much to fathom in Christ, for he is like an abundant mine with many recesses of treasures, so that however deep indi-viduals may go they never reach the end or bottom, but rather in every recess find new veins with new riches everywhere. On this account St. Paul said of Christ; "In Christ dwell hidden all treasures and wisdom" [Col. 2:3]. (C 37.4)

And since love never wanes in its intense desire to know the beloved more intimately:

The soul, then, longs to enter these caverns of Christ in order to be absorbed, transformed, and wholly inebriated in the love of the wisdom of these mysteries. (C 37.5)

The more intimately the bride knows the Bridegroom the more sensitive she becomes to the foul smell of evil; and to see her own failures in love and all the brazen flaunting of the world's sin is a deep pain to her. She agonizes over the rejection of the love of Christ and at the sight of the whole divine order of creation, once established for our good, now violently convulsed: the Shoah, the Gulag, the madness of all cruelty and injustice stoking the overhanging threat of nuclear holocaust. Through this pain she shares in the suffering of Christ and the world ("his heart an open wound of love") and discovers in this suffering a new way of knowing him, a new thicket of Wisdom. There, while she mourns, she learns of the merciful love of God for which no evil is ever too great. Only by entering this mystery of Christ's saving cross of suffering can her desire to descend always deeper in search of the profundities of divine Wisdom be relieved.

**Suffering is the means of her penetrating further, deep into the thicket of the delectable Wisdom of God. The purest suffering brings with it the purest and most intimate knowing . . . because it is a knowing from further within. (C 36.12)**

## The Holy Spirit as Dowry

As the longing for God increased through the anointings of the Holy Spirit, the desire of the soul during the spiritual betrothal to give back to the Bridegroom as much as he was giving to her intensified. John's principle is that "lovers cannot be satisfied without feeling that they love as much as they are loved." So he explains that the soul's growing aim was a love equal to God's love. But even though her love was immense, she felt that it was a languid love when compared to the perfection of God's love for her. She needed to be able to love God mightily with the same strength with which God loved her.

What could she do? Along with her inheritance she receives another gift. As bride she receives, from the Father and the Son, the Holy Spirit as a dowry, now her own possession. She can then love through the Holy Spirit, who supplies her with the strength she lacks. The Holy Spirit becomes for her the love by which she now loves, actually showing her how to love as much she is loved. Thus she loves purely, freely, and disinterestedly, but also now with the very strength with which God loves her. Without this gift the soul could not find complete satisfaction in loving.

The reason the soul desired to enter these caverns was to reach the consummation of the love of God . . . that is, to love God as purely and perfectly as he loves her in order to repay him by such love. . . . This strength lies in the Holy Spirit in whom the soul is there transformed, for by this transformation of glory he supplies what is lacking in her, since he is given to the soul for the sake of the strength of this love. Even in the perfect transformation of this state of spiritual marriage, which the soul reaches in this life, she superabounds with grace and, as above, loves in some way through the Holy Spirit who is given to her [Rom. 5:5] in this transformation of love. (C. 38.2-3)

Because the soul in this gift to God offers him the Holy Spirit, with voluntary surrender, as something of its own (so that God loves himself in the Holy Spirit as he deserves), it enjoys inestimable delight and fruition, seeing that it gives God something of its own that is suited to him according to his infinite being. . . . And God, who could not be considered paid with anything less, is considered paid with that gift of the soul; and he accepts it gratefully as something it gives him of its own. In this very gift he loves it anew; and in this re-surrender of God to the soul, the soul also loves as though again.

A reciprocal love is thus actually formed between God and the soul, like the marriage union and surrender, in which the goods of both (the divine essence that each possesses freely by reason of the voluntary surrender between them) are possessed by both together. They say to each other what the Son of God spoke to the Father through St. John: "All my goods are yours and yours are mine, and I am glorified in them" [John 17:10]. In the next life this will continue unintermittently in perfect fruition, but in this state of union it occurs, although not as perfectly as in the next, when God produces in the soul this act of the transformation.

Clearly the soul can give this gift, even though the gift has greater entity than the soul's own being and capacity; for those who own many nations and kingdoms, which have more entity than they do as individuals, can give them to whomever they will. This is the soul's deep satisfaction and happiness: To see that it gives God more than in itself it is worth, the very divine light and divine heat that are given to it. It does this in heaven by means of the light of glory and in this life by means of a highly illumined faith. (F 3.79–81)

In another text John explains more explicitly how the bride, assumed into the trinitarian life, shares Christ's own breathing forth (spiration) of the Holy Spirit.

No knowledge or power can describe how this happens, unless by explaining how the Son of God attained and merited such a high state for us, "the power to be children of God," as St. John says [John 1:12]. Thus the Son asked of the Father in St. John's Gospel: "Father, I desire that where I am those you have given me may also be with me, that they may see the glory you have given me" [John 17:24], that is, that they may perform in us by participation the same work that I do by nature; that is, breathe the Holy Spirit. And he adds: "I do not ask, Father, only for those present, but for those also who will believe in me through their doctrine; that all of them may be one as you, Father, in me and I in you, that thus they be one in us. The glory which you have given me I have given them that they may be one as we are one, I in them and you in me; that they may be perfect in one; that the world may know that you have sent me and loved them as you have loved me" [John 17:20–23]. The Father loves them by communicating to them the same love he communicates to the Son, though not naturally as to the Son, but, as we said, through unity and transformation of love. (C 39.5)

John daringly states, then, that the Holy Spirit elevates the soul sublimely and informs her (that is, the Holy Spirit becomes the form of her love) and makes her capable of breathing in God the same spiration of love that the Father breathes in the Son and the Son in the Father. The Holy Spirit who is breathed out by the

Father and the Son breathes out to her uniting her to himself. If this statement strikes us as extravagant, John himself is the first to acknowledge that it seems incredible. But he was made experientially aware of its truth in the divine communication to him of this reality: in a moment of actual union within the spiritual marriage. He finds his scriptural backing in St. Paul (Gal. 4:6) and in St. John's Gospel (17:26). His experience of the spiritual marriage in this life gave him a distant taste of what our union with God will be in the next. In addition, the book *De Beatitudine*, which John thought was a treatise by Aquinas, also supported his opinion in expounding on the work of the Holy Spirit in the perfection of glorious love.

In the end, John of the Cross is a witness to the enormous human ability "to taste and see the goodness of God" and affirm that God exists in the incomprehensible mystery of communion among persons. He found the record of God's self-revelation replete with images, metaphors, and narratives about the divine relationship to us and chose those same figures to express his own experience and teaching, but he did so as an act of praise that places his reader in the presence of the living God. To be redeemed means that our unprosperous and bare life be caught up in Christ, caught up in the path of glory. In his *Romances* and in that chapter from St. John's Gospel that he so loved, the Father and the Son glorify each other. John of the Cross urges his readers as followers of Christ to enter into this doxology not only in prayer, but with their whole lives, to "do everything for the glory of God." This is the voice of jubilation that is so sweet to both God and the soul.

Since the soul rejoices in and praises God with God himself in this union, it is a praise highly perfect and pleasing to God, for a soul in this state of perfection performs very perfect works. This voice of jubilation, thus, is sweet both to God and to the soul. As a result the Bridegroom declared: "Your voice is sweet" [Song 2:14], that is, not only to you but to me as well, since through union with me you sing for me—and with me—like the sweet nightingale. (C 39.9)

The two times this saintly friar actually did bring a work of his to conclusion, he ended in a doxology. The *Spiritual Canticle,* the work to which he devoted the most time, ends with this prayer of praise:

May the most sweet Jesus, Bridegroom of faithful souls, be pleased to bring all who invoke his name to this marriage. To him be honor and glory, together with the Father and the Holy Spirit, *in saecula saeculorum.* Amen. (C 40.7)

# Selected Bibliography

*English Translations*

*The Complete Works of Saint John of the Cross.* Translated and edited by E. Allison Peers, from the critical edition of Silverio de Santa Teresa. New ed., rev. 3 vols. Westminster, Md.: Newman Press, 1953. Reprinted in 1 volume, New York: Sheed & Ward, 1978.

*The Collected Works of St. John of the Cross.* Translated by Kieran Kavanaugh and Otilio Rodriguez. Rev. ed. by Kieran Kavanaugh. Washington, D.C.: I.C.S. Publications, 1991.

*John of the Cross: Selected Writings.* Edited with introduction by Kieran Kavanaugh. Preface by Ernest Larkin. Classics of Western Spirituality. Mahwah, N.J.: Paulist Press, 1987.

*The Living Flame of Love: Versions A and B.* Translated with introduction and commentary notes by Jane Ackerman. Medieval and Renaissance Texts and Studies. Binghamton, N.Y.: State University of New York Press, 1995.

*The Poems of Saint John of the Cross.* Translated with introduction by Willis Barnstone. New York: New Directions, 1972.

*The Poems of St. John of the Cross.* Translated by Roy Campbell. Preface by Martin D'Arcy. London: Harvill Press, 1951.

*The Poems of St. John of the Cross.* Translated by John Frederick Nims. 3rd ed. Chicago: University of Chicago Press, 1979.


*Biographies*

Bruno de Jésus-Marie. *Saint John of the Cross.* Edited by Benedict Zimmerman. New York: Sheed & Ward, 1932.

Crisógono de Jesús Sacramentado. *The Life of St. John of the Cross.*
Translated by Kathleen Pond. London: Longmans, Green,
1958.

Hardy, Richard. *Search for Nothing: The Life of John of the Cross.*
New York: Crossroad, 1982.

Ruiz, Federico, and others. *God Speaks in the Night: The Life, Times,
and Teaching of St. John of the Cross.* Translated by Kieran
Kavanaugh. Washington, D.C.: I.C.S. Publications, 1991. The
best all-around biography of John and an excellent introduction to his person and writings.

*Studies*

Arraj, James. *St. John of the Cross and Dr. C. G. Jung.* Chilioquin,
Ore.: Tools for Inner Growth, 1986.

Burrows, Ruth. *Ascent to Love: The Spiritual Teaching of St. John of
the Cross.* Denville, N.J.: Dimension Books, 1987.

Collings, Ross. *John of the Cross.* Way of Christian Mystics 10.
Collegeville, Minn.: Liturgical Press, Michael Glazier, 1990.

Cummins, Norbert. *Freedom to Rejoice: Understanding St. John of
the Cross.* San Francisco: Harper & Row, 1992.

Dombrowski, Daniel A. *St. John of the Cross: An Appreciation.*
Albany: State University of New York Press, 1992.

Doohan, Leonard. *The Contemporary Challenge of John of the Cross:
An Introduction to His Life and Teaching.* Washington, D.C.:
I.C.S. Publications, 1995.

Foresti, Fabrizio. *Sinai & Carmel: The Biblical Roots of the Spiritual
Doctrine of St. John of the Cross.* Darlington Carmel, England:
Darlington Carmel, 1981.

Gaudreau, Marie M. *Mysticism and Image in St. John of the Cross.*
New York: Peter Lang, 1976.

Giles, Mary. *The Poetics of Love: Meditations with John of the Cross.*
New York: Peter Lang, 1986.

Kinn, James W. *Contemplation 2000: St. John of the Cross for Today.*
Petersham, Mass.: St. Bede's Publications, 1997.

Lyddon, Eileen. *Door Through Darkness: John of the Cross and*

*Mysticism in Everyday Life.* Hyde Park, N.Y.: New City Press, 1995.

Matthew, Iaian. *The Impact of God: Soundings from St. John of the Cross.* London: Hodder & Stoughton, 1995.

Merton, Thomas. *The Ascent to Truth.* New York: Harcourt Brace, 1951.

Muto, Susan. *John of the Cross for Today: The Dark Night.* Notre Dame, Ind.: Ave Maria Press, 1991.

————. *John of the Cross for Today: The Ascent.* Notre Dame, Ind.: Ave Maria Press, 1991.

————. *Words of Wisdom for Our World: The Precautions and Counsels of St. John of the Cross.* Washington, D.C.: I.C.S. Publications, 1995.

Payne, Steven. *John of the Cross and the Cognitive Value of Mysticism.* Norwell, Mass.: Kluwer Academic Publishers, 1990.

Payne, Steven, and others. *John of the Cross: Conferences and Essays.* Carmelite Studies 6. Washington, D.C.: I.C.S. Publications, 1992.

Perrin, David Brian. *Canciones Entre El Alma Y El Esposo of Juan De La Cruz: A Hermeneutical Interpretation.* San Francisco: Catholic Scholars Press, 1996.

Rees, Margaret, and others. *Leeds Papers on Saint John of the Cross.* Leeds, England: Simba Print Ltd., 1991.

Sammut, Pius. *God is a Feast: A New Look at St. John of the Cross.* Luton, Beds, England: New Life Publishing, 1996.

Tavard, George. *Poetry and Contemplation in St. John of the Cross.* Athens, Ohio: Ohio University Press, 1988.

Thompson, Colin. *The Poet and the Mystic: A Study of the Cántico Espíritual of San Juan de la Cruz.* Oxford, England: Oxford University Press, 1977.

Poslusney, Venard. *Attaining Spiritual Maturity for Contemplation According to St. John of the Cross.* Locust Valley, N.Y.: Living Flame Press, 1973.

Stein, Edith. *The Science of the Cross.* Translated by Josephine Koeppel. Washington, D.C.: I.C.S. Publications, 2000.

p75

Welch, John. *When Gods Die: An Introduction to John of the Cross.*
    Mahwah, N.J.: Paulist Press, 1990.
Wojtyla, Karol. *Faith According to Saint John of the Cross.* San
    Francisco: Ignatius Press, 1981.

Eph 2:10 For we are God's workmanship,
created in Christ Jesus to do good works
which God prepared in advance for us to do.

p121 Love in aridity can be more intense
    than love in ecstasy

144 perfection of intellect, memory & will in

150-152 vs. 158 I don't understand the
    difference: <u>discernment</u>

193 **rind**
198 Ps 62:1-2
201 Spiritual death
202 Spiritual betrothal